COMMONPLACES

SUNY Series in the Sociology of Culture
Charles R. Simpson, Editor

COMMONPLACES

Community Ideology and Identity
in American Culture

David M. Hummon

State University of New York Press

Cover photo courtesy of the Sheldon Swope
Art Museum, Terre Haute, Indiana. Grant Wood, *Spring in Town.*

Published by
State University of New York Press, Albany

For information, address State University of New York
Press, State University Plaza, Albany, N.Y., 12246

Library of Congress Cataloging-in-Publication Data

Hummon, David Mark.
    Commonplaces : community ideology and identity in American culture
  /   David M. Hummon.
       p.   cm.—(SUNY series in the sociology of culture)
    Revision of thesis (doctoral)—University of California, Berkeley, 1980.
    Includes bibliographical references.
    ISBN 0—7914—0275—4.—ISBN 0—7914—0276—2 (pbk.)
    1. Cities and towns—United States—Public opinion.   2. Community—
Public opinion.   3. Public opinion—United States.   I. Title.
II. Series.
HT123.H86 1990
307.76'0973—dc20   89—36199
                                                                           CIP

10   9   8   7   6   5   4   3   2

For Pat

Contents

Tables, Figures, and Exhibits

Tables

Figures

Exhibits

Preface

People talk a good deal about communities. Personal introductions are often followed by the question, "Where are you from?" or "Where do you live?" Newcomers to a community actively query neighbors and friends about schools, grocery stores, restaurants, and parks, while old-timers brag about a revitalized downtown or reminisce about "the way things used to be." People sometimes debate the virtues of communities, insisting on the superiority of New York over Los Angeles, or city life over small-town life. Community talk even extends to our fantasies and fictions, as we await the news from Lake Wobegon, "where all the women are strong, all the men good-looking, and all the children above-average" (Keillor, 1985).

Such conversations certainly occur for a variety of reasons. People may talk about communities because the topic is relatively accessible to a wide range of individuals. One does not need a doctorate in physics to discuss the energy of big city life. Personal experience and popular urban imagery—from "Lonesome Cowboy" to "Annie Hall"—furnish most individuals with more than sufficient matter. Moreover, many commonplaces about community are relatively innocent. Unlike abortion and gay rights, the risks of offending another through such discussions are relatively low and, with a few queries, knowable. Like chitchat about the weather and pets, community talk often makes suitable discourse for ritual sociability, providing a common ground on which people can meet and exchange the necessary pleasantries of daily life.

Talk about communities also exists because it is essential to understanding the spatial organization of social life. To negotiate the rounds of routine existence, people need to know the location of significant people, organizations, and activities, and they need to situate their behavior in terms of the social norms appropriate to different places. Though much knowledge of the "where" of everyday activity becomes taken-for-granted by the individual, it is nonetheless critical to the successful completion of daily life. The importance of such knowledge is indicated by the various ways it is transmitted: parents informally instruct children; neighbors and work associates pass on community lore; real estate agents and chambers of commerce sell community information; signs, maps, local newspaper features, and guidebooks publicly proclaim their messages.

The ubiquity of talk about communities, however, suggests that such discourse may have more fundamental significance, rooted neither in the logic of sociability nor the spatial structure of daily life. Commonplaces about communities may well represent a fundamental way that Americans conceptualize and interpret society and the self. From this perspective, such conversations are not simply about passing-the-time-of-day nor only about where-things-are. Rather they represent one way—and a distinctly important way in American culture—that people make sense of reality. Here, talk about small towns becomes a way of characterizing a way of life, and discussions of urban crime involve commonsense theories of how society works. Here, debates about suburbs and cities involve deeper commitments to competing values, and questions about where one lives become queries about who one is. From this interpretive stance, widespread talk about communities suggests the centrality of community ideology and identity in American culture.

In developing this approach to the study of community commonplaces, I have had much help. I am deeply indebted to those residents of northern California who willingly gave of themselves to talk with me about their sense of community life in America. Their openness, honesty, and thoughtfulness inspired me to take community talk seriously and, in doing so, pushed me to develop my ideas far beyond what I had originally envisioned.

At the University of California, Berkeley, where this work began as a doctoral dissertation in sociology, others played important roles. Claude Fischer, my thesis chair, has given unwavering support to this project from its earliest beginnings to its fruition as a book. By contributing the professional insights of an urban sociologist and by encouraging my explorations beyond the boundaries of traditional urban social psychology, his efforts have exemplified the role of a mentor at its best. Charles Glock and Gerald Berreman (anthropology), who also served on my thesis committee, furnished useful reaction throughout the dissertation enterprise. Leo Lowenthal, though not directly involved in this project, provided intellectual inspiration for a study of meaning at a time when the sociology of culture was not so fashionable. And graduate student compatriots contributed through discussions, criticism, and good fellowship: Jeff Johnson, Karl Kreplin, Carol Silverman, Joyce Bird, Kathy Gerson, Jane Grant, Sidney Halpern, Robert Jackson, Robert Mayer, and Anne Stueve.

In more recent years, others have contributed greatly. Lyn Lofland has provided invaluable support not only through several readings of drafts but also by helping me to "make connection" with other professionals interested in matters of community belief and sentiment. Her professional and personal efforts exemplify how the ideal of a community of scholars can become a vital reality. Other scholars have furnished thoughtful reaction to varied chapters of the manuscript: Stephen Ainlay, Irving Allen, Irwin Altman, Lee Cuba, Sylvia Fava, Amos Rapoport, Royce Singleton, and Victoria Swigert. Thanks are also due to Holy Cross College for sabbatical support, and to Gary Hamilton and the sociology department of the University of California, Davis, for furnishing a sabbatical home-away-from-home in which to revise much of this book. Ann Papagni, the sociology staff person at Holy Cross, has been an unflappable ally, working and reworking the manuscript through various incarnations.

Pat Taylor, to whom this book is dedicated, deserves special thanks. Her reactions to fuzzy ideas, her insistence on good prose, and her careful editing of the manuscript have no doubt made the book more effective. Her patience, moral support, and love have made it possible.

Part I

Introduction

--- Chapter 1

Community Perspectives:
Community Ideology and American Society

> Human thought is consummately social: social
> in its origins, social in its functions, social in
> its forms, and social in its applications. At
> base, thinking is a public activity—its natural
> habitat is the houseyard, the market place, and
> the town square.
>
> Clifford Geertz,
> The Interpretation of Cultures, 1973.

Page Smith (1966), the historian of small-town America, proposes that American literature was a chronicle of the town until well into the twentieth century.[1] From Harriet Beecher Stowe to Thomas Wolfe, novels and short stories were often set in the town; community life was frequently a central theme of the narrative. Smith argues that authors drew on the image of the town not only because it reflected their own and their reader's experience but also because the town was a powerful symbol for American life. Unlike their European counterparts, for whom social class provided the guiding metaphor for characterizing manners, morals, and daily life, American writers turned to the town again and again to portray the meaning of the American experience.

Like so many other provocative claims of the small town in America, Smith's assertion of the town's leading role in American literature may well be exaggerated. Yet, the thrust of his argument is insightful. Americans—whether novelists or ministers, farmers or bankers—have repeatedly used place imagery to describe, and often argue about, American life.

From Puritans to policy makers, Americans have debated the significance of regional differences, whether contrasting the wilderness and the "the city on the hill," the East and the frontier, the North and the South, or the frostbelt and the sunbelt. Through local boosterism, community promoters have created a rich vocabulary of local identities, celebrated and expressed in community landmarks (San Francisco's Golden Gate Bridge), nicknames (the Big Apple), and such popular paraphernalia as bumper stickers and postcards. (In my hometown of Worcester, Massachusetts, T-shirts proudly proclaim, "Wustah—Paris of the 80s!") As types of places, communities are extolled as distinct ways of life and idealized in the popular iconographies of the New England town, the Midwestern main street, the California suburb, and the towered, city skyline.[2] Even neighborhoods are well represented in the place language of American culture, with recurring exposés of the Gold Coast and the slum, the Upper West Side and the South Bronx. In building and rebuilding American society, Americans have repeatedly transformed the American landscape. In this historical process, they have created a culture exceptionally rich in place imagery, language, and consciousness.

This book is an extended essay on one facet of this consciousness—of the ways that contemporary Americans think and feel about cities, suburbs, and small towns as forms of community. In one sense, then, this work explores the commonplaces of community discourse. Drawing upon depth interviews with residents of a central city, a rural small town, and two metropolitan suburbs, I describe how people talk about the community in which they live and the type of place it is. I report how people who enjoy one form of community think about other types of places: how small-town enthusiasts depict the city; how city fans characterize suburb and town. I document how people conceptualize and explain community problems: why cities have more crime than other places. I recount how people understand their relation to different forms of community and, in some cases, construct a sense of identity as a city person, a suburbanite, a small-town person, or a country person.

As such, this book should interest both lay and professional students of community life. Anyone who has ever wondered about how people in *that type of community* could ever stand, let alone enjoy, living *there* will find an answer to his or her musings. Here, urban planners and policy-makers can explore popular attitudes about communities that influence decision-making in contemporary American life, while community scholars can survey the patterns and sources of community belief and sentiment.

At the same time, this book offers an interpretation of American culture by treating such commonplaces of community belief in an uncommon way: as facets of competing community ideologies. I propose that conceptions of community life are fundamental elements of American culture, with a history and a life that transcends the experience of the individual. I analyze how such conceptions are organized in American culture into distinct community ideologies, systems of belief that define a unique perspective on the landscape of urban, suburban, and small-town life. I argue that people, in adopting such ideologies, incorporate assumptions, beliefs, and values that enable them not only to understand this or that locale but also to *make sense* of reality and their place in the everyday world.

As such, this essay should interest those whose prime concern lies with the interpretation of beliefs and values in contemporary American culture. Scholars in the American Studies tradition, who have investigated the changing role of place imagery in literature and popular culture, will find traditional concerns addressed in a new context. Sociologists of culture will be sensitized to an important, though little investigated, source of meaning in contemporary American life. And all Americans who wish to consider how their consciousness is informed, enriched, and shaped by the implicit structures of their symbolic world will find much to ponder.

Commonplaces about Community Belief

Most Americans enjoy talking about communities. Ask your friends about cities, for instance. They will probably be happy to tell you about the city and the problems of urban life. Between comments on urban crime and the difficulties of raising children in the city, they may intersperse some thoughts on city people, suggesting that urbanites are less friendly and neighborly than other people. Most likely, your friends will volunteer that they do not like cities very much, except for an occasional trip for a baseball game or an evening out at a Chinese restaurant. Or if one of your associates is a city enthusiast, he or she may proudly claim to be a "city person": an individual who enjoys and needs the stimulation of urban life.

Although most people hold definite views about cities, suburbs, and small towns, relatively few individuals give much thought to the origin and nature of their beliefs and feelings. To the extent that people do, they are likely to regard their attitudes toward communities as a relatively direct product of community experience and a simple reflection of "the way places are." As a result, they may regard their views somewhat contradictorily, either as a product of common sense (that which is "naturally" apparent to "everyone") or as a unique outcome of life experience, a biographical collage of Rockford and the Windy City, summer camp and home. Such interpretations are partial at best because they fail to capture the profoundly social nature of popular belief and sentiment about cities, suburbs, and small towns. Community beliefs, I propose, are best understood as interpretive, socially-shared perspectives, learned from community ideology and socially-structured experience.

From Experience to Enculturation

To some extent, our knowledge of communities, both as particular places and as forms of social life, originates in simple, direct experience with places. Children, when asked to draw a map of their world, sketch the immediate environs of home and neighborhood, re-creating their patterns of movement to and from school (Gould and White, 1986). Adults, moving to a new community, learn both the particular contours, sounds, and smells of the new landscape and the spatial organization of community life as they commute to work, seek out stores and places to play, and participate in other activities of local life. If this move involves a new form of community (e.g., from a town to a city), they may learn new ways to act by observing "how people do things around here": whether or not to greet people on the street, when is the proper time to eat. Anyone who has ever created a faux pas in a new community, missed a turn on a freeway, or been lost in the "wrong part" of town knows the potential power of our experiences with community, and that we can—and often do—learn from our personal explorations.

However important such direct experiences may be, much knowledge of communities—and our feelings for them—is learned from the cultural surround of our social world. Such beliefs are taught in the lifelong process of enculturation by family and friends, local institutions, and the mass media. Parents teach children about neighborhoods by stressing where it is safe to play; they instruct on differences between country and city life through reading fables about "country mice and city mice."[3]

Local institutions—newspapers, real estate agents, chambers of commerce—make it their business to teach about communities, often extolling the virtues of the local community and decrying the limits of other places. And in modern American society, the mass media continually saturate the individual with images of places, as sit-coms, advertisements, and popular songs communicate their messages through the symbolism of community settings. The rural simplicity of Walton's mountain and the urban craziness of "Night Court," the country toughness of a Marlboro man and the urban sophistication of a *New Yorker* model, the down-home call of John Denver's "Country Roads" and Lou Reed's invitation to an urban "Walk on the Wild Side"—all are part of the larger symbolic landscape of community life in contemporary American society.[4]

This cultural mediation of attitudes toward communities suggests several ways that experience plays a much more limited—and often ambiguous—role in our understanding of communities than is usually assumed. First, we certainly know and feel much more than we have directly experienced. Whether or not we have ever visited Manhattan, we know about the Big Apple from uncle Frank's tale of his vacation adventure, the I-Love-New-York advertising campaign, and Woody Allen's "Manhattan." The importance of such knowledge is readily apparent in a simple reflection: even though we may never have spent more than a few hours in some form of community, we are often absolutely convinced that such places constitute "the end of the world" and that we would never want to live in such a locale. Second, we actively consult the cultural wisdom of community lore as we take on new places. We use maps and road signs to avoid being lost, and we read the implicit cultural messages in housing styles, neighborhood landscaping, and other built form to evaluate "what kind of place this is" (Rapoport, 1982b; Hummon, 1988). We ask neighbors and work colleagues to find out what is "worth seeing" and experiencing. We consult Miss Manners (Martin, 1979) to find out appropriate ways of behaving in the city: how to deal with urban sidewalk pamphleteers, noisy apartment neighbors, and waiting in lines.[5]

Most importantly, we continually draw upon learned beliefs about communities to interpret our ongoing experience with community. We may note from direct observation that people in a large city are less likely to talk with other people on the street than are people in a small town. How we understand this behavior—whether we "see" it as symptomatic of the rudeness of city people or the wonderful privacy of city life—depends less on personal observation than on the images of urban life that we bring to such experience.

From Reflection to Construction

Though common sense suggests that community beliefs simply "reflect the way places are," this view, too, is inadequate. To the extent that popular beliefs involve empirical descriptions of the way communities work, many popular beliefs are relatively accurate, though even this is not always the case. Popular imagery of urban life, for instance, frequently depicts the city as a place of isolation and loneliness (Strauss, 1961), and Americans, when queried in opinion surveys, are likely to subscribe to the belief that urbanites have fewer friends than other people (HUD, 1978; National Rural Electric, 1968). Sociological research on friendship networks, however, fails to confirm this view: urbanites are just as likely as rural and small-town Americans to have vital networks of friends (Reiss, 1959; Fischer, 1982). Similarly, the physical concentration of poverty in the city, made visible and salient by media coverage and political debate, has led many Americans to identify problems of poverty and unemployment primarily with urban life. Yet rural America has had a higher proportion of poor people than urban America throughout most of this century (Dillman and Tremblay, 1977). Or many Americans believe that the population density of cities—urban crowding—

causes city residents to commit crimes, although there is little empirical support for this view (Fischer, 1984).

More often, the cultural beliefs that people adopt about different types of communities contain the proverbial element of truth. They are, however, highly evaluative and selective in their portrayal of community life, involved in promoting or denigrating a place as much as "describing" it. People may learn that small towns are peaceful—or boring; that suburbs are clean—or sterile; that cities are hectic and overwhelming—or lively and exciting. Such community imagery, by providing a distinct construction of community, suggests that much community belief is fundamentally interpretive, involved in a presentation of reality rather than a simple "reflection" of reality. As Anselm Strauss (1961) has proposed, communities are profoundly *symbolic locales*, places subject to divergent rendering. As we shall see, people who are fond of small-town life describe small towns as ideal communities, easy-going places, where family, religion, neighborliness, and friendship still thrive. To Americans less favorably inclined, small towns are viewed as dreary places—provincial backwaters, filled with gossipy, narrow-minded people. Even widely shared conceptions of communities may foster as much dissent as agreement. Although it is a commonplace that small towns are places where "everybody knows everybody," this "fact" may be given completely different meanings, symbolizing either the warmth of community or the heat of social pressure.

From Individual to Group

Because people's beliefs about communities are to a large extent learned from others through enculturation, people's attitudes toward communities are seldom unique, nor are they universally known. Rather, their views tend to be patterned, shared with others with whom they live and communicate; different from others who lie outside the boundaries of common culture and experience. This is, of course, to some extent a matter of degree. Each person's knowledge and feelings about places are in part distinctive, reflecting the biography and personality of the individual. And a few beliefs about communities are very widely held, traditional elements of culture that may span societies and even centuries. Hadden and Barton (1973), for example, have argued that the antiurban images of the city as a place of moral decline and injustice are central to Western culture, voiced in Old Testament portrayals of Sodom and Gomorrah and contemporary exposés of urban problems.

The social patterning of popular belief and sentiment is nonetheless real, and it can be dramatic in cross-cultural contrasts, where membership in different societies involves enculturation to divergent interpretations of community life. For instance, citizens of France and the United States are likely to express different attitudes toward cities because conceptions of urban life differ in French and American culture. In France the historical association of dominant elites and institutions with cities, particularly Paris, has meant that French culture has developed a strong, favorable ideology of city life. As a result, the French are more likely than Americans to identify the city with "the good life": contemporary opinion surveys indicate that more French people wish to live in cities than currently reside in them. In the United States—where elites have often had rural backgrounds; where dependent, stigmatized groups from foreign immigrants to contemporary Third World minorities have been identified with cities—favorable urban ideology is less developed and less prevalent. In this cultural context, Americans frequently adopt unfavorable views of urban life: opinion surveys show that more Americans currently reside in cities than wish to live there.[6]

Such socio-cultural patterning of community belief and sentiment is also apparent within contemporary American society, particularly along lines of community residence. Though we shall see that other social cleavages such as class and race play a part in the patterning of popular attitudes about communities, present and past residence in different forms of community provides the most important social and symbolic context in which people learn what communities are "really like." Thus, if Americans are less likely than French people to love cities, some—particularly urban Americans— do express prourban sentiments. Though opinion surveys document that fewer than one in ten rural, small-town residents would ideally prefer to live in a large (4%) or medium-sized city (5%), such surveys also indicate that the majority (54%) of residents of large and small cities prefer urban life to other types of places (HUD, 1978). Communities—in part because they shape experience, more because they influence the ideological context in which experience is interpreted and evaluated—profoundly shape popular belief and sentiment about locality in American society.

Perspective, Ideology, and Society

In this book, then, I offer an interpretation of popular belief and sentiment about communities that stresses the cultural and social construction of such views. To capture this complex reality I situate individual belief in the context of both shared symbols and community life. I argue that people, learning about communities, develop what Shibutani (1955) has called a *perspective:*

> An ordered view of one's world—what is taken for granted about the attributes of various objects, events, and human nature. It is an order of things remembered and expected as well as things actually perceived, an organized conception of what is plausible and what is possible; it constitutes the matrix through which one perceives his environment. The fact that men have such ordered perspectives enables them to conceive of their ever changing world as relatively stable, orderly, and predictable. As Reizler puts it, one's perspective is an outline scheme which, running ahead of experience, defines and guides it.

Most of the time, people are not conscious of their community perspective, though these taken-for-granted frameworks shape their understanding of community experience and influence their action toward communities. Such perspectives do not simply "reflect" the way places are; they are best understood as a construction of—an argument about—the way places are. Though used and expressed by individuals, these perspectives are profoundly public: learned, shared, and sustained through communication with others.

At the same time, I propose that community perspectives must be understood in the cultural context of *community ideologies.* Community ideologies are systems of belief that legitimate the social and psychological interests of community residents through their presentation of community life and

people. Like other ideologies, they accomplish these functions through symbolic work: by categorizing, characterizing,
and explaining reality in ways that produce and legitimate
commitment to a form of community. In adopting the beliefs,
values, and assumptions of community ideology, individuals
construct a perspective that makes their community the locus
of the good life. In doing so, they learn a shared way of thinking that makes their community the "best place to live."

Finally, I will suggest that both shared perspectives and
cultural ideologies must be situated in the *social context
of community life*. Though community ideologies are rooted
in American culture as a whole, they play a significant role in
the symbolic life of community, providing a shared framework
for community interaction, defending community interests
against those of other forms of place.

These arguments are developed in the following stages.
"Minding Community" (chapter 2) provides a systematic theoretical and methodological rationale for the approach taken in
this book. It first examines previous work on community belief and sentiment in the social sciences and humanities, suggesting the contributions and limitations of work on mental
maps, community imagery, and studies of community satisfaction, attachment, and preference. It next proposes an alternative conceptualization of community ideology as a cultural
system and lays out a basic conceptual vocabulary for this approach. Finally, in light of this conceptual reorientation, the
chapter provides a brief rationale for the research strategy
used in this study: depth interviews within a comparative
framework of communities. (I provide a more extended discussion of the actual research process on which this book is
based in the appendix, "Researching Community Ideology: Reflections on Method.")

Part 2 addresses the symbolic landscapes of three dominant forms of community ideology: "Small-Town Ideology"
(chapter 3), "Urban Ideology" (chapter 4), and "Suburban Ideology" (chapter 5). Drawing on previous writing and depth interviews, these chapters document how enthusiasts of each
form of community appropriate community ideology to construct a distinct perspective on urban, suburban, and small-
town life—a shared symbolic landscape that legitimates their
affection for city, suburb, or small town.

Part 3 documents further ways that contemporary Americans use community ideology, extending our understanding of the functioning of these ideational systems. "Community Apologetics" (chapter 6) analyzes how contemporary Americans use community ideology to frame and account for "community problems." It demonstrates how the shared perspective of community ideology facilitates the construction of explanations that further legitimate commitment to community. "Community Identity" (chapter 7) addresses how some Americans draw upon community ideology to construct a sense of community identity as an urban, suburban, small-town, or country person. This analysis proposes that community ideology facilitates the characterization of self by defining appropriate qualities for self-conception as a type of person and by articulating ties to community that engender a sense of belonging.

"Community Ideology and American Culture" (chapter 8) concludes with a comparison of urban, suburban, and small-town ideology, highlighting both the substantive differences in values in these varied ideological traditions and the formal similarities in the symbolic, social, and psychological work they accomplish.

Chapter 2

Minding Community:
The Interpretation of Community Belief and Sentiment

> We have emphasized that sociologists have rarely taken the images that people have of the city as proper subjects for sociological study.
>
> Peter Langer,
> "Sociology: Four Images of Organized Diversity," 1984.

> Practically everyone seems to give local sentiments and culture passing attention, but that is usually the end of it.
>
> Gerald Suttles,
> "The Cumulative Texture of Local Culture," 1984.

In chapter 1, I proposed that popular belief and sentiment about community life are best understood through a theoretical perspective that enlarges and, in some respects, contradicts our common sense view of such matters. As befits a sociologist interested in both community and American culture, I suggested that popular views of community life should be interpreted within the context of shared beliefs about places and that such beliefs, in turn, are sustained and have meaning within social groups. This theoretical orientation leads away from the assumption that popular belief and sentiment about places simply reflect personal experience to an interpretation that stresses the public, collective, and symbolic character of community belief and sentiment.

In this chapter, I will develop this argument by moving in two opposite, though complimentary, directions. On the one hand, I will broaden this discussion by examining widely disparate scholarship on community belief and sentiment in the social sciences, humanities, and design professions. Although this interdisciplinary excursus leads off the main track of my central argument, it clarifies important similarities and differences between this study and previous research, and it points the way to fruitful scholarship beyond the boundaries of this work. On the other hand, I will narrow my argument by examining community ideology. Here, I indicate how this central theoretical concept helps to frame my research agenda, and I briefly describe the specific techniques used to develop the materials reported in this work.

Interpretation: An Interdisciplinary Excursus

The wide assortment of studies on popular belief and sentiment about communities makes any attempt at systematic review both difficult and perilous. Like the dinner host who carefully arranges guests around the table to facilitate conversation and avoid conflict, one runs the considerable risk of misplacing authors and work, creating more confusion than understanding. Some such discord is in fact likely: scholars working in different disciplinary traditions approach our intellectual feast with widely different motives and intellectual manners. Nevertheless, I would like to cast previous research into six broad areas, which though not discrete, do differ significantly in three important ways.

First, some studies focus on popular interpretations of *particular communities*, while others investigate popular views of different *forms of community*. For instance, one may investigate either how people evaluate their residential locale as a specific place to live or how they judge towns and cities as alternative forms of community life. This distinction is not always precise in practice. For example, historians interested in attitudes toward urban and rural life in the nineteenth century have frequently turned to popular characterizations of particular communities to infer more general conceptions of community life.[1] More often than not, however, scholars have emphasized one or the other of these concerns.

Second, previous studies frequently differ in their emphasis on people's *knowledge* of communities or their *feelings* for communities. Such phenomena are related: how people think about places can elicit or legitimate sentiment, and emotions certainly shape the formulation and acceptance of belief (Tuan, 1977). Typically, however, research traditions have given analytic precedence to one or the other element—for example, focusing on people's understanding of the spatial structure of a community in one instance and on their emotional ties to community in another.

Finally, in those studies that offer explanations for variation in popular orientations toward community, research differs dramatically in the attention given to *environmental, psychological, social,* or *cultural* factors. Such variation in interpretive context is most often the result of disciplinary perspectives. To some extent, however, these differences have also been shaped by preferences for particular *research techniques* that are more or less conducive to the investigation of different sources of community belief and sentiment.

How, then, have scholars interpreted the way people think and feel about communities? I turn first to four approaches that explore how contemporary Americans view the specific community in which they reside, emphasizing, in turn, spatial cognition, community evaluation, community sentiment, and community symbols.

Popular Views of Particular Communities

COMMUNITY AS SPATIAL ENVIRONMENT: MENTAL MAPS

> There are as many different images [of the city] as there are people. Each is unique, some are directly contrasting, and all serve as guides to people's thoughts about, and behavior within, the cities they encounter.
>
> Edward Krupat,
> *People in Cities*, 1985.

Mental map research is certainly the most well-known work that addresses how people think about the places they

live and work (Goleman, 1985). These studies investigate
how individuals develop simplified "mental maps" (or other
psychological constructs) of the environment, whether that
environment is conceptualized as a room or dwelling, neighborhood or community, region or country. In the research process, local residents are typically asked to sketch their
neighborhood or community, and these "mental maps" are
then analyzed individually and collectively to gain a better understanding of the place as subjectively perceived.[2]

Several disciplines have contributed to the growth of mental map research. Environmental psychologists, interested in
the cognitive processes of spatial and other environmental
learning, have studied mental maps to analyze how the individual constructs a knowable and workable environment
(Moore, 1979). Behavioral geographers, wishing to develop
more accurate theories of environmental behavior, have
turned to mental maps to substitute "real life" thought processes for the normative, rationalistic assumptions of traditional decision-making theory (La Gory and Pipkin, 1981).
Environmental planners have seen such maps as a possible
planning tool, helpful for critically assessing how the built environment is actually perceived by users, providing information that could be beneficial to the design of more humane
environments (La Gory and Pipkin, 1981; Lynch, 1984).

Kevin Lynch's (1960) seminal work, *The Image of the City*,
is suggestive of these concerns. As an urban designer, Lynch
was interested in whether and how the built environment
might facilitate—or impede—the ability of urbanites to orient
themselves spatially within the urban landscape. In a simple,
comparative study, Lynch asked middle-class residents of
Boston, Jersey City, and Los Angeles to sketch a map of their
community. Through an analysis of their "mental maps," he
found that the physical structure of the city—its street patterns, monuments, neighborhoods, and other aspects of the
built environment—did, in fact, influence the ability of residents of different cities to create a coherent image of the city's
spatial structure. Moreover, in demonstrating that some communities are more "imageable" than others, he also suggested
that people use a simplified set of schema to organize their
spatial knowledge—one involving paths, nodes, landmarks,
edges, and districts. Mental maps thus suggested the need for

an environmental psychology in which the spatial and built environment at once "mattered" and was also subject to cognitive interpretation by the individual.

Research on mental maps has expanded this program in a number of directions (Rapoport, 1977; Canter, 1977; Krupat, 1985; Gould and White, 1986). Two are particularly notable in this context. First, though research on mental maps has tended to emphasize developmental and environmental sources of such cognitive images, scholars have also examined the influence of social life on mental maps, producing a social psychology of cognitive imagery. Here, individuals who share membership in social groups or strata are thought to develop similar maps because common social position, with its attendant roles, leads to shared environmental experience.

Long-term residents of a community, for instance, are not only likely to have more detailed and complex maps than newcomers; research suggests that the organization of the image changes, adding spatial knowledge of places to earlier mapping based on route and sequence (La Gory and Pipkin, 1981; Moore, 1979). Gender, with its attendant inequalities and spatial differentiation of behavior, also shapes mental maps. Compared with men, women are more likely to use the home as a spatial reference point, more likely to have a developed conception of the local neighborhood, but less likely to have an extensive conception of the community as a whole (Krupat, 1985).

Class, race, and ethnicity also condition mental maps, with more privileged groups in American society typically creating maps that are more extensive and complex. Such differences may be dramatic where patterns of residential segregation create strong differences in spatial behavior. Peter Orleans, for instance, documented these effects among Anglo, Black, and Spanish-speaking residents of Los Angeles. When asked to sketch maps of Los Angeles, white middle-class residents routinely drew complex, detailed, and extensive maps of the Los Angeles area, linking different parts of the metropolitan area through the web of freeways. Chicano residents, however, and to a lesser extent black residents, typically drew much simpler, localized maps, focusing on the segregated neighborhoods in which they live and those islands in the city socially accessible to each group—for example, downtown and the bus depot (Gould and White, 1986).

Comparative research by Don Appleyard in Ciudad Guay-
ana clearly indicates that such class and racial differences in
mental maps are due to behavioral rather than cognitive or educational differences. In this Latin American city, the spatial
patterns of residence require poor people to travel extensively
through the city, while well-to-do individuals carry out their
lives in more restricted neighborhoods. This patterning, re-
versing the typical segregation of American metropolitan life,
produces correspondingly reversed mental maps: poorer residents draw more complex and extensive maps than do more
privileged urbanites (Krupat, 1985).

Second, in attempting to describe underlying psychological schema that structure environmental knowing, some researchers have shifted their analysis from the spatial imagery
of mental maps to the verbal patterns of linguistic constructs.
Lowenthal and Riel (1972), for example, investigated the language people use to describe the community landscape. To do
so, residents of New York, Boston, Cambridge, and Columbus,
Ohio, took walks through selected urban environments in
their respective cities and then described what they had seen
and experienced. Each city elicited somewhat distinct characterizations of environmental qualities, indicating significant
differences in environmental character among places. At the
same time, residents of all places tended to describe their cities along similar dimensions. Such environmental descriptions not only noted the presence or absence of activity
(moving, noisy) and the spatial orientation of the setting (hor-
izontal, open), but they also frequently emphasized highly
evaluative terms (pleasant, natural). Such language under-
lines the extent to which people inevitably conceive of places
in terms of their value for them: popular characterizations of
communities implicitly and inevitably involve judgments of
communities (Krupat, 1985; Canter, 1977).

COMMUNITY AND QUALITY OF LIFE: COMMUNITY SATISFACTION

There are occasions when the physical sur-
roundings become an important determinant of
behavior, when we hope to enhance our lives by
changing our physical circumstances. But it is
also true that we have a remarkable ability to
adapt to the peculiarities of our environment
and that most of us can learn to live with the

situation we find ourselves in. We not only live
with it, we can be satisfied with it.

Agnus Campbell,
The Sense of Well-Being in America, 1981.

Investigations of the way contemporary Americans judge
their residential communities have increased dramatically
during the last decade and a half. These studies, which have
typically examined people's satisfaction with their local neighborhood or community, have developed from two rather different sources.

On the one hand, scholars concerned with the relationship of community life to policy and planning have become
more sensitive to the fact that the judgments of community
residents about places are often not those of professionals or
policy-makers. For instance, Gans's ethnographic research on
Boston's working-class West End (1962) and suburban Levittown (1967) documented that communities that upper middle-
class professionals (and other outsiders) considered "slums"
or "tacky wastelands" were often valued highly by their residents. Conversely, planned communities and developments,
even when considered models within the design community,
sometimes generated little enthusiasm from their residents.[3]

On the other hand, social psychologists interested in the
quality of life in American society as it is defined and experienced by the individual have addressed community satisfaction as part of their larger research agenda (Campbell,
Converse, and Rodgers, 1976). These scholars have argued
that a person's sense of well-being, whether with family, work,
community, or other facets of life, cannot be understood as a
direct product of the material conditions of his or her life, but
must be interpreted in light of the way the individual perceives
and judges those circumstances. Such perceptions and judgments, in turn, are influenced by learned expectations, values,
personality and other social psychological processes (Campbell, 1981).[4]

Through their use of large, sample surveys, these social
psychologists have helped to describe the broad contours of
community satisfaction in contemporary American society
and the environmental, psychological, and social sources of
such satisfaction. National sample data from 1978, for example,
indicates that three out of four Americans (78%) report they

are satisfied with their community.[5] Though seemingly high in absolute terms, such levels of satisfaction with community are comparable to the way Americans rate other areas of life: approximately equal to their satisfaction with work, housing, and life in the United States; somewhat lower than their evaluations of their marriage or family life; somewhat higher than their ratings of income and their educational attainment. Such satisfaction levels also indicate the general tendency of people to evaluate their life conditions—whatever their objective circumstances—in favorable terms (Campbell, 1981).

Though many Americans report they are satisfied with their community, it is still the case that they are not all equally enthusiastic about the particular place in which they live. Significantly, the type of community in which one resides is associated with community satisfaction. For instance, research comparing residents of central cities with those of suburban communities in forty-six metropolitan areas demonstrated lower levels of satisfaction among urbanites, especially in cities in the New England and the North Central regions (Guest and Lee, 1983). Moreover, national sample data indicate that levels of satisfaction rise as one moves from urban to rural communities. Where only one in five (20%) central city residents report they are completely satisfied with their community, nearly half (48%) of residents of rural areas do so (Marans and Rodgers, 1975; see Dillman and Tremblay, 1977; Campbell, 1981; HUD, nd; Christenson, 1979). Americans of different social backgrounds also differ in their satisfaction with their community, though such differences are not great and, to some extent, they are inconsistent between studies. Nevertheless, people who are satisfied with their community are more likely to be white, older, long-term residents, and middle-class (Campbell, Converse, and Rodgers, 1976; Fried, 1982; Hunter, 1974; Marans and Rodgers, 1975).[6]

Community satisfaction research has been less successful in explaining such differences in levels of satisfaction, though suggestive work points in several directions. First, one might argue that urban, suburban, and rural residents differ in their satisfaction because people of different social backgrounds tend to reside in different community forms. White, as opposed to black, Americans tend to live in suburban or rural locations, and white Americans are more likely to be satisfied with their community. However, the notable differences in community satisfaction voiced by urbanites, suburbanites, and rural residents are not largely due to these differences in the social composition of community forms (Rodgers, 1980; Marans and Rodgers, 1975).

Second, objective conditions of the community—in terms of both the built and social environment—do influence community satisfaction, but there is considerable disagreement as to the precise role that such conditions play. For instance, people who own their own home, live in larger residences, and have friends living in the local area are more likely to evaluate their neighborhood favorably (Guest and Lee, 1983). Higher levels of neighborhood satisfaction among white and middle-class Americans appear attributable to the better residential quality of their built environment (Fried, 1982).

At the same time, the influence of such objective features is largely mediated by people's perception and evaluation of features of their community. People who are satisfied with their community tend to rate it more highly in terms of particular attributes: the public schools, police-community relations, local taxes, and the climate (Campbell, Converse, and Rodgers, 1976). Similarly, people who are satisfied with their neighborhood are more likely to believe that their local area has good neighbors (friends and socially homogeneous), a safe, clean environment, and good housing (Guest and Lee, 1983). Such individual beliefs, when compared with objective, independently measured community differences, largely account for explainable variation in community satisfaction. This suggests that objective features of the community— whether social or environmental—do influence community satisfaction, but they do so only to the extent that they are meaningful to the individual—that is, marked out, evaluated, and interpreted (Campbell, Converse, and Rodgers, 1976; Miller, Tsemberis, Malia, and Grega, 1980).

COMMUNITY SENTIMENT: ATTACHMENT TO PLACE

> An elderly woman exemplified this . . . when she spoke almost tearfully about the neighborhood where she had raised her family: "It makes me sad; it's a slum now, but I still love it!"
>
> Albert Hunter,
> *Symbolic Communities*, 1974.

If mental map and community satisfaction research have respectively conceptualized the local community as an object of spatial cognition and evaluation, other scholars have treated community as an object of sentiment—a spatial and social locus for feelings of the individual. Though sharing concerns with studies of community satisfaction, this work is distinct both in its conceptual emphasis on the emotional investment or attachment of the person with place and in its theoretical origins in social theory (Hunter, 1978). Sociologists, particularly, have pursued this matter because the way contemporary Americans feel about their residential communities is entwined in one of the central questions of community and urban sociology: What is the social and psychological significance of place in modern, urban society?[7]

For social theorists of the nineteenth and early twentieth century, the emergence of modern society inevitably meant a decline in the significance of local forms of social organization and a concomitant erosion of both social and sentimental ties to place. The social forces that undermined community attachment differed from theorist to theorist. For Marx, capitalism transformed the traditional relations of people and place into market relations, ultimately substituting a cash nexus for the traditional social bonds that tied peasant to lord and both to land (Marx, 1972; see Engels, 1968). For Durkheim (1969) and Weber (1946, 1958), the increasing division of labor and the emergence of modern bureaucracy diminished all forms of primordial ties to land, locality, and family, substituting more formal, contractual, and temporally limited social bonds guaranteed by the nation-state.[8]

In the middle decades of this century, this theoretical legacy provided the central paradigm for much work in urban and community sociology. Louis Wirth (1938), in his classic statement, "Urbanism as a Way of Life," argued that the increasing scale and complexity of city life weaken the primary ties and local sentiments of the urbanite, creating a person at once more cosmopolitan and rational and more disengaged and blasé. Students of the American community from the Lynd and Lynd (1929) to Vidich and Bensman (1960) documented the transformation of the rural community by national economic life, mass culture, and the growing power of state and national government (see Martindale and Hanson,

1969). Such arguments, emphasizing the "decline of community," more often than not underlined purported negative consequences of weakened local ties: increased crime, deviance, and general social disorganization; rising anxiety and placelessness for the individual.

Though powerful, this "decline of community" literature has come under frequent attack during the last two decades for a wide variety of reasons. Both historical research and theoretical explication indicate the inadequacy of the perspective's unilinear and typological model of change and decline (Fischer, 1977; Gusfield, 1978). Moreover, several empirical literatures suggest that the thesis's view of people's eroding sentimental attachment to place is at best too simple.

Ethnographic studies of local neighborhoods and communities indicate that some people do have significant social ties to places and that these, in some cases, nourish emotional attachment to those places. Studies of working-class urban neighborhoods (Gans, 1962; Young and Willmott, 1957; Kornblum, 1974; Rivlin, 1982; Steinitz and Solomon, 1986) and of rural communities (Coles, 1967; Erikson, 1976; Peshkin, 1978; Cochrance, 1987) demonstrate that local areas can be a continuing locus of sentimental identification. Moreover, if such attachment is broken through forced relocation by community change or natural disaster, individuals may experience considerable grief and psychological loss (Fried, 1963; Erikson, 1976).

Though such studies suggest that local sentiment has not evaporated in the heat of mass society, one could argue that such pockets of place attachment are simply "residuals" of older community forms. However, other research, utilizing systematic surveys, also indicates that community and neighborhood sentiments are more complex than the traditional decline-of-community thesis would imply. People's social ties to places appear quite variable, depending on both a variety of social (e.g., life cycle) and place (e.g., housing quality) characteristics, and these, in turn, influence sentimental commitment to place.

For instance, these studies indicate that psychological attachment to community has different dimensions, and that the attention given to community satisfaction has captured only one element of people's feelings about a locale (Kasarda and Janowitz, 1974; Gerson et al., 1977; Guest and Lee, (1983).

Though people's sentimental attachment to a locale (as empirically measured by a willingness to leave a place or a "sense of
belonging") tends to be associated with community satisfaction, this is not always the case. People may evaluate a place
in relatively unfavorable terms and feel considerable attachment to the locale.

Moreover, sentimental attachment to place, unlike "community satisfaction," is not strongly associated with different
forms of community, either for rural-urban (Kasarda and
Janowitz, 1974) or central city-suburban (Gerson, et al., 1977)
comparisons. Differences, where noted at all, are quite weak
and mixed: people in smaller places are slightly more likely
to feel a sense of belonging but not more likely to say they
are unwilling to move. Such cross-sectional persistence of
community sentiment across community forms does not,
of course, "disprove" the decline of community thesis; yet it is
certainly not the pattern of sentiment that one would expect
from the traditional thesis.

Finally, sentimental attachment is influenced by objective
features of both the built and social environment. Home own-
ership and housing quality (as independently assessed) are
associated with greater psychological attachment to neighborhood and community (Gerson, et al., 1977; Guest and Lee,
1983). Long-term residence in a place also increases the likelihood of expressing sentimental ties to place, primarily
because long-term residents are more likely than newcomers
to have local social ties of friend and kin (Gerson, et al., 1977;
see Kasarda and Janowitz, 1974; Hunter, 1974; Guest and
Lee, 1983).

COMMUNITY AS TEXT: READING LOCALES

> The city, then, sets problems of meaning. The
> streets, the people, the buildings, and the
> changing scenes do not come already labeled.
> They require explanation and interpretation.
>
> Anselm Strauss,
> *The Image of the City*, 1961.

Scholars concerned with the local culture of community
life provide a final perspective on the way contemporary Americans think and feel about their communities. Like other re-

searchers, these scholars argue that popular views and sentiment are not a simple reflection of community conditions. Unlike others, they stress the importance of shared beliefs and
values in shaping popular orientations, rather than emphasize mediation by psychological or social processes.

From this perspective, popular views of communities are
not regarded as simply—or perhaps even primarily—a matter
of "subjective" individual experience. Rather they are always
seen in the context of cultural forms that are thought to define the identities of communities and people's feelings about
local life. As a result, this work has most often examined community icons, slogans, and other forms of local culture: such
extrinsic sources of meaning are regarded as the critical
means through which people conceive and interpret their
community. In this view, local residents draw upon local culture to give a "proper reading" to their community, frequently
relying on such ideological defenders of local culture as journalists to provide authoritative community imagery. Here, residents "read" the community landscape, interpreting the
social and symbolic messages encoded in the styles and other
features of the built environment. Here, local groups within
the community sometimes engage in ideological conflict over
the meanings of places.[9]

Several studies provide evidence for this position by doc-
umenting the role of local culture in the symbolic construction of the identity of a community (Suttles, 1984; Strauss,
1961; Lofland and Lofland, 1987; Tuan, 1974; Karp, Stone, and
Yoels, 1977). Suttles (1984) examines how large cities—New
York, Chicago, San Francisco—accumulate rich local traditions that define and celebrate the distinct character of place.
Community slogans and bumper stickers, landmarks and
statues, myths about community founders and leaders—all
contribute to a collective definition of locality. As collective
representations come to have a life of their own, they are further elaborated and defended by local journalists and other
boosters. As representations, they simultaneously serve to in-
tegrate the local life of the community and to advance the economic and political interests of the city in regional and
national competition.[10]

Such battles over the meaning of places also occur on
a smaller scale. As Krase (1979) has noted, the identity and
reputation of an inner-city neighborhood is not simply given

in its housing or residents but is defined, in part, through on-going ideological conflict over the meaning of the place. Thus, although national culture often stigmatizes such inner-city neighborhoods as not only environmentally but morally deficient, community activists may provide counterclaims that stress the vitality of their local areas. Through community associations, house tours, historic preservation, local parades, street banners, and other symbolic activity, residents may work to enhance the visibility and reputation of the local area.[11]

Within the city, local culture is also significant in defining and sustaining the spatial structure of the community. In separate studies of Chicago and Seattle, Hunter (1974) and Guest and Lee (1983) have documented the persistence for over a half-century of symbolically defined local areas. Such continuity suggests that people's conceptions of neighborhood structure are grounded in shared culture rather than individual perception. This view is further reinforced by Hunter's (1974) investigation of the social factors that influence knowledge of neighborhood structure. In his study of residents of Chicago, people who were able to name and define the boundaries of their local area were those who were most likely to be adept at local knowledge: long-time residents and members of community organizations.[12]

Popular Views of Forms of Community

Two disparate traditions contribute to our understanding of the way Americans think and feel about urban, suburban, and small-town life as forms of community. On the one hand, scholars of American culture and community life have examined the portrayal of urban, suburban, and town life in popular and elite culture. Such secondary analyses of community imagery are typically interpretive, often historical, and frequently quite valuable in suggesting the deeper cultural conceptions that underlie popular belief and sentiment.

On the other hand, contemporary social scientists have directly examined popular belief and sentiment about communities through social surveys. Most often, such work focuses on community preferences, asking Americans where they would reside if they could live anywhere they wished. A few studies also directly ask individuals to evaluate specific differences between different forms of communities. Such work has its origins in public opinion polling, though it has received considerable attention from demographers and community sociologists interested in questions of mobility, migration, and the policies affecting population dispersion (Zuiches, 1982). With notable exceptions, this work tends to be descriptive, suggesting broad patterns and social correlates of individual belief and sentiment.

COMMUNITY AS PUBLIC OPINION: COMMUNITY PREFERENCES

> Research interest in residential preferences emerged in the early 1970s, the result of a puzzling discrepancy between attitudes and behavior. Several national polls had shown that most Americans, if given a choice, would live in a rural place.
>
> James J. Zuiches,
> "Residential Preferences," 1982.

Community preference research provides three important insights into the structure and sources of popular orientations toward community life. First, these systematic surveys indicate that people tend to prefer the type of community in which they reside—it is the modal choice (HUD, 1978; see Mazie and Rawlings, 1972). To some, the fact that people tend to equate the type of community in which they reside with the ideal form of community may not seem remarkable. Yet this finding does contradict two frequently heard claims: that *all* Americans idealize some particular form of community (typically the small town or suburb); that preferences simply reflect the objective characteristics of communities.

Several different processes may contribute to the tendency of Americans to prefer the type of community in which they reside. This may simply reflect a psychological movement toward consistency in which people transform necessity into a virtue in order to avoid frustration. People with distinct community preferences may also sort themselves into their preferred forms of community over time through a general process of community mobility. Some research by behavioral geographers suggests that discrepant preferences may play a limited role in determining both the likelihood and destination of migration (DeJong and Sell, 1977; Zuiches and Rieger, 1978; Zuiches, 1982).

Communities, as cultural contexts, may also shape preferences through socialization. Community studies, for instance, have documented how small-town parents, through the selection of school boards, teachers, and curriculum, transmit a favorable image of small-town life to their children (Peshkin, 1978). Preference studies indicate, thus, that childhood residence in a city, suburb, or town increases the likelihood that a person will see that form of community as ideal as an adult (Zelan, 1968; Mazie and Rawlings, 1972; HUD, 1978; Howell and Frese, 1983). Moreover, parents, when asked where they would ideally like their children to reside when grown, are likely to select the form of community in which they currently reside (HUD, nd).

Finally, as a result of such socialization, residents of different forms of community may prefer different types of places because they conceive of them differently. For instance, though 69 percent of town and country residents believe that rural areas have the friendliest people, only 34 percent of city residents agree (HUD, 1978). Although 42 percent of town and country residents are sure that the best schools are located in nonmetropolitan areas, only 20 percent of suburban and 12 percent of city residents concur (HUD, 1978). Moreover, people who prefer urban residence over other places tend to think about their preferences differently, basing them on considerations of higher wages, better jobs, and social diversity, rather than considerations of crime, environmental quality, and children (Fuguitt and Zuiches, 1975; see Blackwood and Carpenter, 1978). Such fragmented work implies that residents of different forms of communities come to prefer the type of place in which they reside because they have learned to think about their form of community in favorable ways. This possibility is indirectly but dramatically supported by a recent study that examines the changing beliefs of young Americans who have moved to New York City after having been raised in suburban communities (Fava, 1984). These urban migrants, it was found, were frequently distinguished by having spent extended but temporary periods of time in cities prior to their move—time in which they "relearned" their sense of what cities are and might be.

Second, public opinion studies indicate that American community preferences, when viewed collectively, are somewhat "antiurban" in their structure (Campbell, 1981). Although many Americans are fond of the type of place in which they currently live, many others would rather live in some other type of community. More often than not, those with wanderlust choose a smaller, less-urban place. For instance, the U.S. Census (1987) estimated that 25 percent of Americans lived outside central cities or suburban areas in 1980. Throughout the 1970s, opinion surveys reported that anywhere from half to two-thirds of the population would ideally prefer to live in a small town or the rural countryside (Mazie and Rawlings, 1972; HUD, 1978). Such comparisons surely exaggerate the magnitude of unfulfilled (prorural) preferences: careful studies also indicate that the majority of people who say they want to live in a small town or the countryside wish their community to be within relatively close proximity to a city (Fuguitt and Zuiches, 1975). Nevertheless, the antiurbanism of preferences is substantial, and there is some evidence to suggest that it has grown during the 1960s and 1970s (Zuiches, 1981).

Public opinion surveys also document that antiurban preferences are matched by other unfavorable beliefs about cities. For example, when asked whether America would be better off without cities, one in ten Americans (11.2%) responded affirmatively and even larger numbers said they were not sure (14%) or did not think it would make any difference (19%). Other unfavorable beliefs about city life are quite widely held. Though not all Americans concur, many charge that cities have the most crime (92%), the worst schools (63%), the worst housing (63%) and are the worst for raising children (83%). Yet, even such widely held beliefs about cities are not uniformly negative, suggesting that many Americans may be ambivalent in their views of cities. For instance, contemporary Americans also suggest that cities have the best cultural opportunities (90%), employment opportunities (72%), health care (73%), and shopping (62%) (HUD, 1978). A recent small-scale survey of college students also reproduces these broad patterns. When students listed characteristics of contemporary cities, frequently volunteered attributes were more often unfavorable than favorable, but the latter were also present

(Krupat, 1985; see Fuguitt and Zuiches, 1975; Blackwood and Carpenter, 1978).[13]

Third and finally, opinion research indicates that people's preferences for communities are shaped not only by their community residence but also by their social position in the larger society. Black and Hispanic Americans, for instance, are more than twice as likely as white and Anglo Americans to say they would like to live in a large city (HUD, nd). Individuals with more education or who work in white-collar occupations are somewhat more likely to prefer to live in a metropolitan city or suburb, and people with very high levels of education may be especially attracted to cities (Gallup, 1971 and 1973; Mazie and Rawlings, 1972; HUD, 1978). Though evidence is limited and contradictory, men may be somewhat more likely than women to prefer rural areas (Fava, 1985; but see Gallup, 1971). People at different stages of the life cycle also report somewhat different community preferences. In all likelihood, young and single Americans are disproportionately attracted to cities; middle-aged individuals with families, to suburbs; and the elderly, to nonsuburban communities (Zelan, 1968; Zuiches and Fuguitt, 1973). Finally, though little evidence is available, religious background may also be associated with different community preferences, with American Catholics expressing more prourban preferences (21%) than Protestants (13%) (Gallup, 1971).

Community preference studies have not, however, adequately specified the varied reasons for these associations between social background and preference for different places. To some extent, these associations may simply reflect the broad social ecology of American society. Residents of large communities, for instance, are not only more likely to prefer cities than people in small places; they are also more likely to be young, single, better educated, more well-to-do, employed in a white-collar occupation, and black (Fischer, 1984).

Such differences in preferences may also be the result of the different opportunities, experiences, and values that such social backgrounds entail. For instance, although the somewhat more prourban stance of black Americans is largely attributable to their relative concentration in central cities, their enthusiasm for cities does not appear entirely attributable to urban residence. Black urbanites are somewhat more prourban in their preferences (64%) than are white city dwellers (51%); among black and white suburbanites wishing to live elsewhere, blacks are almost twice as likely as whites to want to move to a city (23% versus 12%) (HUD, 1978). For whatever reasons—the historical experiences of blacks in the rural south; fears of racial discrimination in housing and employment in predominantly white suburban and small rural communities; the opportunities afforded by a distinctly black urban subculture—black Americans appear to evaluate the city in more favorable terms than their white counterparts irrespective of residence.

COMMUNITY AS SYMBOLIC LOCALE: COMMUNITY IMAGERY

> Without denying the significance of the political, economic, technological, and organizational dimensions of urban problems, we argue that the negative *image* man holds of the city looms as a major obstacle to the maturation of urban civilization. In substantial measure, the discontents of urban civilization are a function of man's deep-seated and fundamental rejection of the city as an *idea*.
>
> Jeffrey Hadden and Josef Barton,
> "An Image that Will Not Die:
> Thoughts on the History of Anti-Urban
> Ideology," 1973.

Scholars interested in the interplay of American culture and the environment have, for some time, investigated the history and symbolism of community imagery. More often than not, these studies have focused on images of the city and urban life, but some investigations have also documented the imageries of suburban, small-town, and rural life. Using novels and newspapers, sermons and advertisements, paintings and photographs, scholars have explored the symbolic presentation of community life in varied media and texts. In doing so, they have clarified how popular belief and sentiment about community are grounded in shared cultural images of community life.

This work enriches our understanding of popular belief and sentiment toward community in a number of ways. Clearly, studies of the cultural record provide our only access to community belief and sentiment in the past, and thus provide critical historical depth to our understanding of the topic. This literature's greatest contribution, however, may lie in its theoretical treatment of popular belief and sentiment. In the best studies, popular belief and sentiment are situated within deeper, systemic, cultural images, and these images, in turn, are placed within the context of social conflict and change.

Specifically, community imagery research indicates that the language and visual imagery of community forms is richly symbolic in American culture. For example, Meinig (1979) has proposed that particular forms of American community life have been richly imbued with connotative meanings. The New England village, as it is idealized and depicted in popular photographs, paintings, and writing, is hardly a simple reproduction of small-town life. Rather, it involves a distinct cultural iconography—Congregational church spire; trim, white houses with metal roofs; colored autumn leaves—that speaks of deeper American values: intimacy, tradition, stability, prosperity, cohesion, and family life.

With such sensitivity to symbolism, scholars of community imagery have also shown how images of community life frequently involve a stance toward community—a sentimental or moral posture toward a way of life. For example, studies of fictional accounts of city life often emphasize that such texts are antiurban in their portrayal of the city as a place of social disorganization, moral decline, corruption, and alienation (Gelfant, 1954). Such a rhetorical stance, communicated through shared antiurban images, may contribute to a deep-seated animus against city life in American society (White and White, 1964; Hadden and Barton, 1973; Tuan, 1974; but see also Bender, 1975; Susman, 1985.)

Such concerns have also meant that image research has emphasized that community belief and sentiment are structured. In one sense, this is implicit in a perspective that interprets popular attitudes in terms of more basic cultural conceptions. Scholars of community imagery, however, sometimes pursue this insight further, suggesting that popular orientations are linked to systems of images. American agrarianism, for instance, does not simply assert the superiority of rural over urban life, but involves a system of beliefs and claims: that rural life is closer to nature, fosters greater independence, supports democratic citizenship, and nourishes moral and religious life (Hofstadter, 1955; see Bender, 1975; Buttel and Flinn, 1975; Furay, 1977; Strauss, 1971).

This concern with the systemic character of community imagery has lead to the identification of possible oppositional structures that frame community imagery in American culture. In a brief review of images of rural versus urban life, Fischer (1984) notes that community imagery has often involved four basic oppositions: nature versus art; familiarity versus strangeness; community versus individualism; tradition versus change. Moreover, because both elements of each opposition can and have been valued by some groups at some times, these oppositions have provided suitable frames for apologists of both rural and urban life. Thus, while rural life is typically identified with nature, familiarity, community, and tradition, and urban life with art, strangeness, individualism, and change, these oppositions often support opposing meanings. For rural apologists, the personal freedom of urban life is expressive of social isolation and a loss of traditional values; for urban apologists, such freedom is a sign of the individualism and creativity of urban life.

Finally, community image research has fruitfully explored how basic cultural images of community life are produced and transformed through social change and conflict. At its best, this work has recognized that the emergence of a new form of community—the industrial city, the suburban development—has engendered problems of meaning as well as more commonly recognized demographic, social, and political conflicts. Old conceptions of community life are no longer adequate to capture new forms of community experience and organization; old metaphors and images no longer reflect the emerging community, class, and other social interests. Thus, literary critics have sensitively analyzed how nineteenth-century novelists (and social critics) provided new and compelling metaphors for thinking about the emerging industrial city (Williams, 1973; Marcus, 1975; Marx, 1968, 1984), while cultural and social historians have fruitfully described the symbolic reworking of community imagery in popular culture (Bender, 1975; Warner, 1984, 1962).

For instance, Warner (1984) documents the language and visual imagery used to depict the "slum" in the industrial city of the nineteenth century and early twentieth century. By tracing the emergence, meaning, and social usage of this new

urban image, he explicates how a new way of conceiving the
city and poverty developed simultaneously over the course of
the century. Moreover, this conceptual posture did not simply
"reflect" environmental change. The image of the slum was
not created by urbanites in general, but by middle-class residents who used this label to designate sections of the city
they thought both undesirable and exotic.[14] Incorporating elements of both liberal and secular middle-class ideology, slum
imagery helped to simultaneously secularize and "environ-
mentalize" middle-class beliefs about poverty, thus shifting
class inequality from the potentially critical discourse of religion and political economy to the everyday language of community forms.

Summary

What, then, does this interdisciplinary excursus of recent
scholarship suggest about our understanding of popular belief
and sentiment about communities? It indicates that we may
well know more about this phenomenon than is typically assumed because good but highly fragmented research has remained unknown to concerned scholars, isolated by the
boundaries of disciplinary specialization and research approaches. This review may also disclose a growing awareness
of the multidimensional character of popular orientations toward places more generally. Such consciousness leads researchers not only to investigate people's spatial conception
or overall satisfaction with their local community but also to
probe deeper into the symbolic meanings and sentimental attachments people have for places.

Most of all, this excursus highlights the complexity of the
sources of popular belief and sentiment toward communities.
The community, as a spatial and built environment, clearly in-
fluences some facets of popular orientations, shaping the im-
ageability of people's mental maps, the satisfaction they
express with their local area. What is striking, however, is the
extent to which these and other facets of popular belief and
sentiment are mediated by social and cultural factors. The
form of community in which one resides—as both a social
and cultural context—shapes community satisfaction and the
type of place one is likely to regard as ideal; one's residential
history alters mental maps, community satisfaction and sentiment, as well as broader community preferences. Social

background—class, race, gender, and life cycle—in turn modify knowledge of the community and broader preferences for forms of community life.

However compelling, this interdisciplinary review also discloses missing elements in scholarship on popular belief and sentiment about communities. Currently, we know more about how people think and feel about particular locales than we do about how they form perspectives on different types of communities. Although there is a growing sensitivity to the symbolic mediation of popular belief and sentiment about communities, we know less about such cultural processes than we do about environmental or social factors. Though previous research repeatedly indicates that the form of community in which one lives is critical to varied aspects of community belief and sentiment, few studies directly explore how communities, as symbolic contexts, shape popular perspectives on community forms. In short, such omissions reveal the need for a close study of community ideology in contemporary American culture.

Community Ideology as a Cultural System

In his famous essay, "Ideology as a Cultural System," Clifford Geertz (1973) outlines a theoretical approach that is appropriate to a study of community ideology as a cultural system. A symbolic anthropologist, Geertz proposes that ideology is a distinct cultural form that serves specific symbolic as well as social and psychological functions. Thus, although ideology certainly legitimates political, class, and other social interests, although it can channel frustration caused by psychological strain, Geertz emphasizes that ideology first provides a symbolic rendering of the world, one that gives concrete form and meaning to life.

This perspective on ideology involves two central ideas. First, like other cultural forms such as religion, myth, art, or science, ideology involves a *way of thinking that is public.* Rather than view thought as a personal process that takes place "in the head," Geertz argues that thought is basically "extrinsic," a process in which individuals draw upon cultural symbols to interpret perception and experience. Culture, through language, ideology, and other ideational systems, thus provides the symbolic resources—the vehicles of conception—through which individuals and groups, more or less successfully, make sense of reality (Keesing, 1981).

Second, ideology, as a public way of thinking, symbolizes reality in a distinct way: it characterizes life in such a way so as to *motivate commitment and action.* Unlike science, whose language and style of presentation portray reality in a "disinterested" manner, ideology, as a cultural system, is rhetorically persuasive: its language—in content and style—frames the world in terms of a stance, or motivation, toward the world. Such symbolic work makes possible the social functions of ideology, when, for instance, a class ideology portrays society in a manner that renders inequality as either beneficial or exploitive, natural or artificial, unchangeable or transitory. Such symbolic work also facilitates the psychological functions of ideology, providing, for instance, a favorable vocabulary of motives for the interpretation of self.

In this light, a *community ideology* may be defined as a *system of belief that uses conceptions of community to describe, evaluate, and explain social reality, and that does so in such a manner so as to motivate commitment to community.* Like other ideologies, community ideologies are ways of thinking: their assumptions, beliefs, and values, involve a particular "vocabulary of discourse" and structure (Perin, 1977). Like other ideologies, community ideology is public. Though individuals adopt and use community ideologies to think about different forms of community life, community ideologies are collective representations, the product of social life and conflict rather than personal experience and imagination. Like other ideologies, they are not disinterested: they symbolize community forms in ways that legitimate social and psychological commitments to a particular form of community.[15]

This theoretical perspective suggests that our primary research task must be to document and interpret how urban, suburban, and small-town ideology provide the symbolic resources that enable people to build and sustain commitments to different forms of community. Empirically, this will entail the interpretation of interviews with people who live in and like different forms of community, an interpretation that suggests how a shared, cultural perspective, drawn from a community ideology, transforms community belief into community commitment. Analytically, this will involve showing that community ideology—whether urban, suburban, or small-town—accomplishes five important symbolic tasks.

Community ideologies enable people to define *what types of places exist,* or, more precisely, they provide individuals with a simple community taxonomy, "marking out" and identifying different forms of settlement for public recognition and interpretation. For example, although city and suburb are separated only by political boundaries and relative location, and although metropolitan suburbs incorporate new housing developments, inundated small towns, and the rural countryside, community perspectives simplify a complex social reality into an abstract scheme of community types, enabling the individual to interpret places through a limited, discrete number of community forms. Different ideologies, moreover, vary to some extent in their community taxonomies. Small-town ideology, as we shall see, does not identify suburbia as a distinct type of community, and, as a result, small-town enthusiasts usually do not "see" suburbs and suburbia as a distinct form of community.

In addition to defining the basic categories of community types, community ideologies characterize the nature of different places through central images of the ideology. The imagery of this descriptive *symbolic landscape* is richest and most complex for its home community, but the ideological perspective also provides a guide to the essential features of other types of places as well. Through urban ideology, urban enthusiasts learn not only about cities and urban life but also about suburbs, suburbia, and suburbanites. Moreover, the ideology provides the landscape with a simple, oppositional (polarized) structure. In general, community ideologies portray the community landscape so that the fundamental imageries of community stand in opposition to each other—their essential characteristics of the home community contrasting sharply with the essential features of other types of communities. For instance, urban ideology portrays cities as liberating places; from this urban image, small towns become places of personal oppression. The central imagery of this landscape, with its oppositional structure, gives the community ideology its interpretive power.

Community ideologies also provide individuals with *community accounts:* popular explanations of differences among communities. People who share a community perspective not only express a common view of what different communities are like but also, through such accounts, share a sense of *why* places are the way they are. Conversely, individuals with different perspectives, even when they agree on some characteristic of place, may differ strongly in their explanation of that community attribute. As we have noted, the large majority of Americans correctly believe that American cities have more crime than other types of communities. As we shall see, however, city and small-town enthusiasts offer a different range of accounts for urban crime and danger.

Community ideologies, like other ideologies, not only present a conceptual landscape of what-places-are-like; they also convey an implicit conception of what *communities ought-to-be-like*. By integrating values into their selective portrayal of the community landscape, community ideologies identify one form of community with the "good life," and relegate other places to a netherworld of community problems. This evaluative process, accomplished through the expressive power of community imagery, ensures that community ideologies are *moral landscapes*, instilling ideological perspectives with moral as well as cognitive authority.

Finally, community ideologies enable some individuals to define a *community identity:* a sense of being a city person, a suburbanite, a small-town person, or a country person. Within the ideological context of a shared perspective on communities, people are able to identify with places—to define ties to a form of community and to construct a sense of belonging in an urban, suburban, or small-town community. And from the imagery of the perspective, people are able to characterize themselves as having particular personal qualities, drawing on shared conceptions of community residents to elaborate conceptions of self.

People and Places: Urbanists, Villagers, and Suburbanists

To explore community ideology and identity, seventy-seven adults were interviewed in four communities in northern California: San Francisco, a central city; Hillcrest, an upper middle-class suburb in the San Francisco metropolitan area; Bayside, a working-class suburb in the San Francisco metropolitan area; and Valleytown, a rural small town in the central valley of California. (The names of the smaller communities are fictitious in accordance with a research protocol negotiated with the Committee on Human Subjects, University of California, Berkeley.) The logic of this design—to interview in depth a relatively small number of individuals within a comparative framework of community forms—is particularly appropriate to the cultural analysis of community ideology and has some distinct advantages over previous research.

Unlike community imagery research in the humanities that relies on cultural artifacts to infer symbolic meanings, depth interviews make it possible to examine popular thought directly and to determine the extent to which general, cultural images actually inform the way people view places. Unlike social survey work on community preferences, depth interviews enable people to convey their community perspectives with spontaneity, detail, and complexity. The use of open-ended questions allows the respondent to define and describe places with little direction. This procedure guards against the research bias of question format, lessening the extent to which people's responses are framed and influenced by the preconceptions of the researcher. Most importantly, this enables adherents of different ideologies to "speak for themselves," using the cultural imagery and vocabulary of their perspective.

San Francisco, Hillcrest, Bayside, and Valleytown provide an excellent comparative framework in which to examine community belief and sentiment. They do not, of course, represent the total diversity of community life in contemporary America, nor can each community be said to be typical of all other communities of its type.[16] This comparative sample, however, does facilitate the documentation of various types of community ideology and, through comparison of these cultural forms, the construction of a more formal, systematic understanding of community ideology (Glaser and Strauss, 1967).

In each community, households were selected randomly from dwelling lists in two or more theoretically chosen neighborhoods. Using census tract data and field observation, middle- and working-class neighborhoods were designated in each community to ensure class diversity within each community type, and Hillcrest and Bayside were included to ensure adequate class variation within the suburban context.

Given the racial segregation of suburban and small-town communities in northern California, the San Francisco neighborhoods selected were composed predominantly of white residents, thus ensuring that urban residents did not differ significantly in minority background from suburban and small-town residents.[17] Households were sent a letter describing the research; up to four visits were made to each household to locate possible respondents, leading to completed interviews with slightly over half of the households.

The interview lasted approximately one and one-half hours and was taped and transcribed with the permission of the respondent. Individuals were queried about their sense of the community in which they were raised and current community of residence; their beliefs about cities, suburbs, and small towns; their community preferences; their sense, if any, of community identity; and their explanations of selected place differences. These topics were covered in the sequence just listed, and questions posed early in the interview were least directive in language and form.

Respondents were diverse in community and social background, with the above-noted exception of race. Urbanite, suburbanite, small-town resident; newcomer and old-timer; young and old; men and women; married couples, widows, singles; middle-class and working-class individuals—all participated in the study.[18] More importantly, this diversity of community and social backgrounds is matched by similar diversity in belief and sentiment about communities. Like Americans in national opinion polls on community preferences, residents of San Francisco, Hillcrest, Bayside, and Valleytown frequently disagree about the ideal community in which to live, and these differences are often marked by community background.

In Valleytown, a substantial majority of the residents interviewed might be called *Villagers:* people who prefer to live in a small town or the countryside (Table 1). These small-town residents are also predominantly antiurban: when asked where they would least like to live, three out of four selected the city (Table 2). In contrast, San Francisco provides a home to a majority of *Urbanists:* people whose ideal place of residence is the city. Finally, though suburban Hillcrest and Bayside are the home of some suburban Villagers and Urbanists, these communities also contain a plurality of *Suburbanists*, for whom the suburb is the locus of the good life.

Table 1: Community Preference by Community of Residence

Community of Residence

Community Preference	San Francisco	Hillcrest & Bayside	Valley-town	
City	62%	15%	0%	(20)
Suburb	4	38	0	(11)
Small Town	12	19	40	(18)
Countryside	23	19	48	(23)
Farm	0	8	4	(3)
Wilderness	0	0	8	(2)
	101%	99%	100%	
	(26)	(26)	(25)	(77)

Table 2: Community Antipathy by Community of Residence

Community of Residence

Community Antipathy	San Francisco	Hillcrest & Bayside	Valley-town	
City	8%	42%	76%	(32)
Suburb	19	4	0	(6)
Small Town	23	8	0	(8)
Countryside	0	4	4	(2)
Farm	19	12	4	(9)
Wilderness	23	31	12	(17)
Can't Say	8	0	4	(3)
	100%	101%	100%	
	(26)	(26)	(25)	(77)

Part II

Symbolic Landscapes

Chapter 3

Small-Town Ideology[1]

Few would argue today that the condition of mental life in the small town is better than in the city, or that there is less alcoholism or a better family situation. There may be greater tranquillity in the small town but no more happiness; there are face-to-face relations but no deeper understanding of the human situation; there is a more compassable universe to grasp, physically and socially, but in reality it is not less bewildering.

Max Lerner,
America as Civilization, 1957.

No small town is exactly like any other; each has its own flavor, intimacy and set of values. Nor can one point to any single factor that makes people return to small towns in ever greater numbers. But from those I talked to, one feeling emerged more frequently than any other: a sense that small towns had been better able to preserve a way of life that Americans had come to cherish.

Roul Tunley,
"The Comeback of the Small Town," 1977.

Small-Town Popularity

Places, like heroes, have popular histories. For a few brief years, they capture the imagination of the popular media, then

47

recede into the taken-for-granted landscape of American society. In the 1950s commentators on the American scene gazed across an expanding metropolitan landscape. Seeing tract housing, station wagons, and organization men, they reacted—most with horror, a few with pride—and contested the meaning of suburbs and suburban life. In the 1960s civil rights protest, the war on poverty, and ghetto revolt shifted attention from the suburbs to the central city, and talk of suburban conformity gave way to cries of urban crisis. In the 1970s the urban Goliath still dominated public attention, but an unlikely David, the American small town, emerged to do battle for the American imagination.

Roul Tunley's article, "The Comeback of the Small Town," published in *The Reader's Digest* (1977), typifies much of what has been written about the small town in the popular press.[2] Tunley suggests that American cities have lost their lure and that Americans are moving to small towns in increasing numbers. To support this contention, he draws upon well-publicized census data, which indicate that nonmetropolitan areas are growing at a more rapid rate than metropolitan areas for the first time in decades. Small-town America, it seems, has been experiencing a revival, brought about by the return of urban Americans to their small-town home.[3]

Tunley reports a number of factors that experts offer to explain this small-town renaissance. Americans are "fed up" with urban problems, and they want communities in which they can control their lives more effectively. Moreover, unlike rural communities earlier in the century, towns are now less isolated from the economic and cultural opportunities of urban America. Tunley then concludes:

> Perhaps more important than any of these reasons is the feeling that most Americans have that we are small-town people at heart. A recent Gallup sampling showed that nearly 90% of Americans would prefer to live in a small city, a town, or village, or in a rural area.

Tunley's claim that most Americans are Villagers at heart is certainly exaggerated, although the fact that the argument is made—and made often in the popular press—is itself indicative of the popularity of the town.[4] As we saw in the previous chapter, many Americans prefer city and suburban communities to small-town residence, and many apparent Villagers are drawn to suburban towns rather than the rural town or countryside. Nevertheless, the claim that the town is a sentimental favorite among Americans does capture an important facet of contemporary community sentiment. As we saw in chapter 2, more Americans would like to live in a small town or the rural countryside than currently do. Small-town residents, more than residents of city and suburb, prefer the type of community in which they live, and they are more likely to report that they are satisfied with the particular community in which they live.

How, then, are we to understand this popularity of the town, a sentimental attraction most notable among small-town residents but not limited to such individuals? Like Tunley, popular writers often initially focus on the objective conditions of the town and argue that, in general, small-town life offers significant advantages over urban and suburban life. Such arguments have some merit, but they encounter two difficulties. Although some differences in the quality of life between types of communities can be assessed more or less objectively, the relative importance of these differences to people is a matter of value. Small towns may afford more access to clean air, hunting, and fishing; cities, to Chinese restaurants and specialized medical services. These differences, however, do not automatically make small towns—or cities—better places unless one or another system of values is adopted.

Moreover, even for those relatively central concerns of life that many Americans would agree are important, small towns—particularly, rural small towns—do not surpass cities and suburbs in any consistent or decisive way, and in many areas of life they are found wanting. Although small towns are generally safer to live in than cities or suburbs, they offer neither the economic, cultural, or medical opportunities of cities, nor the quality of housing, education, or commercial services of suburbs. Although small-town residents are more often satisfied with the community in which they live than are people in other places, they do not appear to be healthier or better psychologically adjusted than city people, nor do they appear significantly happier with their lives in general than people are in larger communities (Dillman and Tremblay, 1977; Fischer, 1984).

Such difficulties lead writers to suggest that the sentimental attraction of many Americans for the town must be interpreted in terms of deeper, underlying motives in the
American psyche—forces that make Americans "small-town
people at heart." In the early 1950s, Max Lerner (1957), for instance, proposed that the continuing attraction of the town is
symptomatic of a search for lost community in modern society. More recently, Peter Schrag (1972) and Richard Francaviglia (1976) speculate that the favorable sentiment for the town
may be driven by a pastoral wish for a simpler, better place
and time. The most sophisticated of these interpretations, offered by Vidich and Bensman in *Small Town in Mass Society*
(1960), argues that the sentimental orientation of Americans
toward the town necessarily involves an idealization of the
town, an idealization fueled by the strains of contemporary
mass society. Small-town Americans, they argue, idealize the
town to displace resentment against their personal and communal dependence on mass society; urban Americans who
idealize the town do so as an expression of their frustrations
with modern urban life.

These arguments may well capture some of the deeper
sources of favorable sentiment for the town, but they also
pose difficulties. Each surely reduces what is a complex pattern of motivation among individuals to a single, dominant
motive—a motive that is very remote from the experience of
the individual and that can be inferred only indirectly. Moreover, while such arguments may have psychological strength,
they are culturally weak. If the town is an appropriate outlet
for emotional yearnings for community, we need to explore
how the town effectively symbolizes community in contemporary American culture. If small-town enthusiasts hold an idealized view of small-town life, we need to understand the
shared ideological images of community life they use to interpret the community landscape.[5]

This chapter examines how small-town enthusiasts draw
upon the shared beliefs and images of small-town ideology to
describe the community landscape of contemporary American
society. Specifically, we will document how Villagers in Valleytown routinely describe life in town, city, and suburb, drawing
on a shared cultural perspective that portrays the town as the
locus of the good life—a place of caring and community, a
simpler world, and a haven from the problems of modern, ur-

ban life. In doing so, I propose, they draw upon a rich and enduring symbolic landscape in American culture, a perspective that reinforces and legitimates their commitment to small-town life.

Valleytown and its Perspective

> We had friends we had met in St. Louis who came to Valleytown for a visit for a week. He had been born and raised in St. Louis. And it was interesting, his reaction. He just couldn't get over it. He'd sit in the backyard—he couldn't fathom the quietness of it. There was a street out in front and there wasn't all the noise from the traffic.
>
> And we leave our front door open in the evening—to get a breeze through. And we'd be in the back part of the house. One night he came back running and said that he'd closed the door for us. And we told him. And he said, "You mean you can sit in the back part of your house and leave the door open?" So far we can.
>
> An to go uptown, and go in and visit with a clerk. My husband took him uptown one day to the bakery. And they went in the backdoor and the baker was still baking something. You knew him. I got some sense of what he felt from being in a small town.
>
> A Villager in Valleytown

Valleytown is a community of 7,500 people located in the San Joaquin Valley in northern California. Founded in the last third of the nineteenth century as a transshipping point from railroad to wagons, Valleytown became an agricultural center in the twentieth century as irrigation brought needed water to the surrounding countryside. Today, as a food processing and service center, its local economy is still dependent on agriculture and the rural countryside, though its residents increasingly turn to employment in urban centers in the region.

Although Valleytown is beyond the daily commuting range of the San Francisco metropolitan area, it is located in a growing agricultural county with a rapidly growing city of 85,000 approximately one-half hour's drive away. In recent years, Valleytown has been growing quite rapidly. From 1900 to 1950 Valleytown grew slowly to a population of 4,000; then in the last quarter of the century it has nearly doubled its population.

Residents of Valleytown and other northern California towns prove no exception to national public-opinion surveys, which show that small-town residents prefer to live in small towns and country settings. A systematic survey study of northern Californians in the late 1970s indicated that small-town residents most often preferred small town (47%) or rural residence (31%) to life in a large city (7%), small city (11%), or suburb (4%).[6] In Valleytown, most of the people with whom I spoke were Villagers, also preferring to live in a small town or the surrounding countryside. Those who did not, wanted to live in even less urban settings, sometimes farms and ranches, a few in the wilderness. Moreover, when asked where they would least like to live, most Valleytowners, without hesitation, specified the city.

These preferences are rooted in the shared perspective of small-town ideology, a collective view with several general features. Most beliefs about small towns are embedded in a more or less explicit contrast to beliefs about cities. A visitor simply cannot talk to Valleytowners about small towns without eliciting contrasting images of the city.[7] At the same time, beliefs about suburbs, suburban life, and suburbanites are not, by and large, part of the symbolic landscape of Villagers. When directly asked about suburbs, most Villagers have little to say; most are vague. Finally, because the perspective draws heavily on small-town ideology, its imagery of the community landscape is highly selective, strongly evaluative, and warmly affectionate toward the town.

The Town as Ideal Community

"WELL, IT'S A QUIET TOWN SINCE IT'S A SMALL TOWN"

When you ask Villagers to describe small towns, one of the first things they are likely to mention is the atmosphere of the town. Often, these characterizations begin with the suggestion that small towns are *"quiet places,"* in some cases literally so:

> Yes, Valleytown is a typical small town. It has a comfortable way of living. For people who would be coming from a large city, small towns have a kind of peace and quiet, and they're away from smog. Life is hectic enough—in a quiet town, the quietness can be good.

More often, there is the characterization of their *slow pace* of life:

> Oh, the attitude of the people, the country living, nobody's in a rush in a small town. And it's quiet: no hurry and go all the time. . . . In cities there's too much traffic for the way I was raised. I can work fast if I have to, but I like to take it easy. Being raised in a country town—going into the city, it's too fast. You live a year in a day and I don't like that.

To most Villagers this "slow, easy-going pace" is a characteristic feature of the town's atmosphere. To many, it also helps to account for a second aspect of the town's atmosphere, its *friendly ambience.* As one working-class man, who had recently moved back to Valleytown, suggested:

> Well, a small town, it just has a slow, friendly-type atmosphere. It doesn't take long to get acquainted with people. A small town seems to be friendlier, and a little more carefree. When I lived in Valley City, it took me four months to get acquainted with my neighbors: they didn't seem to have time for anything but themselves. Around here, I got acquainted with one neighbor in three days.

"IN SMALL TOWNS YOU HAVE REAL NEIGHBORS"

Since the atmosphere of the small town is easy-going, slow, and friendly, Villagers generally assume that it's "normal" for small towns to be *neighborly* places. Like the person quoted above, they often comment that people in small towns usually get to know their neighbors, not like cities, where people "don't even know who lives next door":

> I have sisters who live in Bakersfield—that's a city. And they
> want to get out of there. . . . Down there, they're not friendly.
> She said there was years that they didn't even know who
> lived next door. I know the neighbors here.

Some Villagers also imply that small-town neighborliness
normally includes *mutual concern* in addition to casual ac-
quaintance. The elderly, in particular, were likely to comment
on this:

> In a small town people are more friendly. You have real neigh-
> bors who look out for each other and drop in on each other
> all the time. People are willing to help each other. In San
> Jose there was a neighbor I never even got to know. That's
> not living.
>   In small towns people are more involved with other peo-
> ple. Like in a city, somebody could mug you right out in front
> of your place, and no one would become involved, because
> they don't want to. More compassionate for other people. If
> you see people in trouble, you run and see if you can help
> them. I think that's important.

Yet, younger Valleytowners also commented on the neighborliness of the town and on the callousness of city people:

> I drove a truck down to the city, Friday. Was I glad to get out
> of there, and I was just there one day. I think city people
> think more of themselves than other people. It's like some-
> body surviving: just watch out for yourself. It seemed like no-
> body wants to help you. When you ask for help, it was just as
> if they didn't hear you.

"Being Small, Everybody Knows Everybody"

Perhaps no other image of the town is repeated so frequently as "in a small town, *everybody knows everybody*."
The image is complex, is used in several contexts, and has
several connotations. First, it is important to recognize that
this feature of town life is often viewed as the primary characteristic of the small town. To many Villagers it defines the
small town, providing the social yardstick by which relative
size is translated into a type of place. In Valleytown, a place is
considered a small town, rather than a large town or city, not

because it has a given number of residents but because it is "small enough" for residents "to know one another." To many, it is also essential because it accounts for many other features of the town, from friendliness and neighborly concern to safety and public order:

> People are friendlier in small towns. I think it's the town, itself. In towns things are slower. The people stay, they have roots. Mainly the slow pace, and naturally they're friendlier since they know everybody from somewhere.

When Villagers suggest that small towns are places where everybody knows everybody, they often imply that relationships in the town are *personal, rather than impersonal,* in quality. As already noted, neighbors are not simply people who live next door but "real neighbors." Similarly, store owners and employees are their "friends," rather than shopkeepers; people met on the street are real or potential acquaintances, not simply fellow inhabitants of Valleytown:

> Well, I love the town because I am acquainted with so many people, not really on a social scale, but it's nice to walk down the street and see people that you went to school with, even though you don't any more than say "hello." You don't associate with them socially, but it's nice to know everyone and to know their relatives, and who they married, and their children, and sometimes even their grandchildren.

To some Villagers, of course, this personal quality to social relations is associated with a threat to privacy. In Valleytown "everybody knows everybody" is often rapidly followed by "everybody knows everybody's business." Typically, Villagers joke about small-town gossip and the way "news travels":

> Everybody knows everybody's business. You don't need a newspaper, that's for sure [laughs]. The newspaper is usually just out-of-town news. We get one weekly newspaper and that covers about everything you'd want to know. Everything else gets relayed so fast you don't really need a newspaper.

If gossip is thus a modest source of concern, to most this aspect of town life is "worth the price." For instance, even the Valleytowner I spoke with who was most critical about small

towns—she was often ambivalent—made the following remarks on town gossip:

> What would I say about small towns? Probably all the wrong
> things—I'd tell them all the things I shouldn't tell them.
> Many of the people who came here when we did—we discuss
> the town—and we ask, "Do you suppose all towns this size
> are really like this?" Most people say, "yes," though some
> say, "Good heavens, no, it couldn't be this bad."
>
> Again, if you come to a small town, you've got to expect
> that people are going to be watching and criticizing to your
> face and behind your back. But I guess this is part of life. But
> I see the opposite, too: many people have a real concern for
> you. And that's very good—it's a wonderful thing to experi-
> ence. I would say it's been a really great experience to know
> so many people, all the way from "just-hello-acquaintances"
> to a small number of very close friends.

In Valleytown, "everybody knows everybody" may also imply that there are *no social barriers* to getting to know fellow
residents. Not everybody, in fact, knows everybody, nor could
they.[8] What is essential, Villagers claim, is that anyone could
get to know someone if they wished. In part, Villagers view
this as an aspect of the size of small towns:

> Let's compare newspapers, okay? If you look at the Valley-
> town *Bugle* you know this guy on the front page, or you know
> the different store owners—there aren't that many stores,
> and you can relate to that a lot faster. You say, "Hey, I saw you
> in the paper yesterday." Try that in Valley City or some bigger
> city. Sure you know who your mayor is, but have you ever
> seen him or ever talked to him? I don't know the mayor here,
> but I know other people.

But it may also be used to imply an *egalitarian quality* to
relations among small-town residents:

> You take your little rural towns like Valleytown and Valley-
> dale—everybody knows one another. But in suburbs and cit-
> ies they each have their own little clique. Where in a small
> town, everybody is invited—more or less—to join in, whether
> you know much or not.

"In a Little Town They're More Concerned with Children"

Most residents of Valleytown think of small towns as ideal places for families. They may volunteer that small towns are more *"family oriented"* and that families "stick together" and spend more time together:

> Well, in small towns you probably have more of a home life. Like in our family, we get together about every weekend with my wife's family. And especially during the summer. We have a barbecue almost every weekend. I don't know if they have that in the cities or not, but we have it here.

Most often, when Villagers talk of town life and the family, they speak of children. Nearly everyone with whom I talked in Valleytown believes that small towns are *excellent places to raise children* and that cities are mediocre at best and often very poor. Small towns, they believe, are superior because the physical environment is especially suited to their conception of a child's world. The young, family man just quoted, later added:

> In small towns you can have animals for your kids, things for them to do, like riding bicycles, going to parks, and picnics, as opposed to walking down the pavement to the corner and walking back to the other corner. Of course, if you had a lot of time, you could probably make something for them to do in a city or escape from the city and take a weekend up in the mountains.

Cities, Villagers may note, may have some activities and places for children, particularly parks. But they think these are not easily accessible elsewhere or are just part of the problem:

> Cities are no places for children. In Sacramento, they might have parks, but there are the drunks, the rapists, and sadists, and they come in big towns and go unnoticed.

Finally, most Villagers think that small towns are excellent for children because their friendly atmosphere and social scale make it possible to know—and control—their child's world. In small towns, they suggest, it's easier to keep "track of your child":

> I think the people in small towns are generally friendlier than in your big cities. People don't have time for each other there, while [here] everybody knows everybody else and their children. Like I know with my two children, I know where they are just about all the time. And if I don't know where they are, one of my girlfriends does. It's that simple. If you were in a big community, well, if you don't know, too bad.

And it is also easier to "find out how he or she's doing at school":

> In a small town you can get acquainted with the teachers; maybe know a lot of the families that your children know. The schools are smaller so they can have a better relation with the teacher.

And it is easier to control a child's development:

> You have more children from different types of homes in the cities—you have a cross section that's all thrown together. Children from all walks of life are thrown together and maybe one child picks up traits from another because he gets away with it. In smaller communities you're more aware of what's going on so you can tell your child, "I don't want you going with this or that child." In a larger place, you don't know whether he's been in trouble or not.

"SMALL TOWNS ARE A LOT SAFER THAN CITIES"

Finally, all residents of Valleytown believe that small towns are far *safer* to live in than cities. Many, pointing to the crime and violence they read, hear about, and "see" in cities, contend that cities are not safe to live in. For some, like a woman who had moved with her husband at retirement from the San Francisco area to Valleytown, the safety of the town is a salient characteristic of small places. When asked about small towns, she immediately commented:

There's not traffic congestion in small towns and the crime's low. You're more free—not afraid to walk downtown. If you live in a city, you don't feel safe. . . . We used to go to San Francisco, when we lived in the San Francisco area, to see light opera, but not any more. You can't even walk down the street. The more heavily populated, the worse it gets, and the people change.

Other Villagers, however, take the safety of the town for granted. With their friendly, neighborly atmosphere, small towns can be expected to be safe places. Thus, one working-class man, echoing the sentiments just expressed, said:

In cities, there's too much riff-raff. You have to protect your back all the time. . . . I feel pretty safe in a small town and strictly safe in the wilderness. There's crime in a small town but it's penny ante stuff. Only a few murders once every year or two. In small towns, people control their own. If people are friendly, honest, you shouldn't have any crime. And in a small town, people are concerned.

Cities: The Un-Community

The central images used by Villagers in Valleytown to describe cities and urban life are also, for the most part, drawn from small-town ideology. In most cases, this imagery of urban life stands in opposition to that of the town: the essential features—and vices—of urban life are defined by the virtues of small-town life. As we have just seen, when Villagers describe the town, they inevitably turn to the city to clarify—through contrast—their conceptions of small-town life. Conversely, when Villagers address the topic of the city directly, their presentation of urban life to a large extent reproduces their more implicit indictment of cities contained in their depiction of the town. Thus, when asked to describe cities, Villagers volunteer that cities are *noisy and hectic:*

Cities are noisy and completely different from small towns. In cities it's rush to work, rush home. Then you don't see people anymore. I don't like to be close to my neighbors, but I like to see them, to have a conversation with them.

. . . rushed and uncaring:

The city has too many people, too much going on, all mixed in too fast. City people are too busy doing other things to be friendly. Country people, they sit back and enjoy.

... alien and impersonal:

I don't really have a good sense of what city life is like. I've visited San Francisco, but I would never live there. We just go there to mess around once in a while. It's so cold and impersonal. There, you walk down the street and everybody's checking everybody out. It's strange. You feel everybody's watching you all the time.

... dangerous and no place for children:

Cities are very poor for raising children. There's more violence in cities and more things like drugs. I wouldn't be gullible enough to think that it doesn't go on here at all, but it does much less in a small town than a city. The overall atmosphere means a lot in bringing up my children: the atmosphere of the town, the friendliness, and not having the rat-race type of situation of the city.

In two ways, however, Villagers add to—and in some ways modify—their presentation of the town through their depiction of cities. First, they often propose that cities have a less natural environment than small towns. Villagers describe cities as *dirty and polluted,* and they usually believe this to be the inevitable consequence of the concentration of people, cars, and, in some cases, industry in cities:

Cities have more pollution 'cause of the masses of buildings, masses of factories, masses of people, masses of cars, just masses—total, people, amount, numbers! And I don't think it's just cars; just bunches and bunches of things.

In some cases, however, Villagers attribute the physical condition of the urban environment to a moral impoverishment of urban life:

Generally speaking, cities are a lot more polluted than small towns. Traffic is the main difference, and I think people in the city just don't give a darn. Not just air pollution, but as far as throwing whatever kind of waste material. They don't really give a darn. Maybe it's part of what they've grown up in. You can see people living in homes that are not kept very clean. Growing up in that, in the city environment, it's just not frowned on as much in the city as it is out in the country.

Villagers may also suggest that the city's *inhuman scale and density* makes it less natural than the town. This indictment is often expressed as a personal reaction to the monumentality and density of the city. One young Villager, commenting on his experience of town and city, thus remarked:

I lived in San Francisco and Los Angeles when I was in the Navy, and all that did is just cure me. I don't want no big city. I wanted out from the time I got in. It seems like you're surrounded by the city. I'm not claustrophobic or anything, but it seems like you can't escape from it. To me, being raised in a place where you can look over the back of your house and see the mountains and everything, just seeing more buildings was, you know. . . . I don't like crowded places; that's what it amounts to.

This assessment of urban pollution, scale, and density, when combined with the Villager's other beliefs about urban liabilities, gives the Villager's community perspective its strong antiurban animus. Villagers may, in fact, conceive of cities exclusively as a locus of problems, and, when queried about cities, they may simply offer a catalogue of "urban problems":

Cities, there's the unfriendliness: you can just lie there and die. People need help on occasions. And all the problems: taxes are greater, there's more crime. You're cooped up in your house and yard. And everywhere you look there are people and houses. You can't breathe the air and there's traffic congestion.

There are, however, two facets of urban life—work and play—that generate some disagreement among Villagers. Some people with whom I spoke believe small towns provide excellent economic and recreational opportunities, while others emphasize the advantages of cities in these areas. Socially, these interpretive stances are not sharply drawn, but younger, newer, middle-class residents are more often critical of such opportunities in small towns than are older, long-term, working-class residents. Among those who emphasize the opportunities of the town, Valleytown was characterized as having "what bigger places have." Moreover, its country location was felt to provide a variety of outdoor recreational activities that "cities don't have." For opportunities that Valleytown lacks, these Villagers felt that the town's "closeness to other places" and "its central location" alleviate any problem.[9] When asked to describe what Valleytown was like to someone who wasn't acquainted with it, one woman Villager replied:

> Well, it's a small community. The people are friendly, and it has as much to offer as far as shopping as you would driving to Valley City. Clothingwise, you have a good style line, and costwise, it's just about the same. I think we have just about anything to offer for someone moving or looking the area over.
>
> We have a lot of activity. There's the rodeo and lots of agriculture. And we're close to the junior college in Valley City. And you can travel to the mountains. It's a center location. You have the advantages of your reservoirs and boating activities, and a lot to offer people locally—baseball games, Little League, swimming. We have many churches; the school system—we have grammar schools, junior high schools, and the high school.
>
> And there's the bus to the junior college. And there are work advantages here, not as much as in a larger city, but it is available to those who want to work. And we are growing— we've had a lot more to offer in the last two years than we did previously.

Other Villagers, however, suggest that cities are superior to small towns in the recreational and economic opportunities they offer. They noted that for recreation " you've just got to make a trip to a bigger place once in awhile":

> Small towns don't have much activity—most small communities that I've been in. Sports, anything like that, recreation. We have to go to Valley City. And even five or six times a year, we go up to San Francisco.

And, however begrudgingly, these Villagers volunteer that cities are "better for jobs" than small towns:

> Cities are very hectic, and city people are kind of rude, I think. There's just a lot of noise and confusion, a lot of traffic, a lot of smog. The only good thing about cities is work. There's a lot of jobs, you know. Like if you were looking for work, naturally you would be better off in some place like San Francisco than in Valleytown because you'd have a better chance of getting a job.

The Invisible Suburb

Although small-town ideology provides Villagers with a predominantly unfavorable view of cities, it does not categorize the suburb as a distinct form of community and, as a result, does not provide defining images of suburbia for the community landscape. Consequently, most Villagers, when queried about suburbs, simply had little to say about suburban life, despite the fact that some have lived in places that social scientists would consider suburbs and most have had some contact with suburban life through friends and relatives. The suburb and suburbia simply lack sufficient ideological definition and significance to be incorporated routinely into their descriptions of different types of communities.

When Villagers do talk about suburbs, they must rely on their conceptions of town and city to suggest that suburbs are—in some ways—either like small towns or like cities. Given their polarized interpretation of town and city life, this means that suburbs are either portrayed as predominantly urban places—and hence undesirable—or as villagelike—and consequently somewhat attractive. Villagers *never* describe suburbs as combining the "best of the small town and the city," as is suggested by suburban ideologues, nor are they portrayed as incorporating the "worst of small-town and city life," as some urban critics of suburbia maintain.

Those Villagers who did describe suburban communities most often portrayed suburbs as essentially urban places, hardly distinguishable from cities. For a young Villager in Valleytown, suburbs, like cities, are crowded places:

> No, a suburb is not that different: it would just be an extension of a crowded city to me. They're just trying to get a little

more room. That's about what it amounts to. Where in a
small town or on a ranch, you've got all kinds of room.

To an elderly Villager, suburbs are like cities because they
are both riddled with crime:

There's very little distinction any more between suburbs and
the city. In Stockton and, I think, the Bay Area, there's just as
much violence in the suburbs as in the city. Even more, perhaps, from what I read and what happens. And the people are
more or less the same, hardly any distinction, if any.

Although these characterizations of suburbia link suburbs to cities through such defining characteristics of urban
life as density and crime, Villagers also argue that suburbs are
fundamentally urban because they are inhabited by ex-city
dwellers:

No, I think suburbs take on city ways. Because the people
move out of the city to the suburbs and they bring their traditions with them. They want to have their little town out
there, but I don't think they're getting away. They may be further out, but. . . .

In some cases, however, Villagers note that suburbs are
"more like small towns than cities." As such, they are necessarily preferred over cities; however, even these descriptions
of suburbs lack enthusiasm:

Oh, suburbs are pretty good, a lot better than the city.
They're kind of like small towns, but they're in a chain all
gathered together. But you've got the hassle and the trying to
get in and out of the town—the rat race. Seems like everybody who's got to live in the suburbs has got to work in the
city. Also, in the suburbs and cities, people don't help out as
much. If a guy's got problems, people don't talk with his family. If he's drunk at a bar, nobody helps or drives him home.
It's just none of your business.

At best, suburbs are credited with some of the virtues of
the town and, thus, are thought of by some as a possible alternative to the town:

If I had to live in a city, I would want to live in a suburb—in the suburbs where I could have a yard 'cause I love gardening. Living there would be more the same. You'd have the same type of feeling about your neighbors there as in a small town. Maybe you wouldn't have as much time to spend with them, because of the commuting. But in your yard, that's where you'd get to know your neighbors.

The Symbolic Landscape

In fellowship! I think that in this simple emotion lies my joy in living in this, my village. Here, this year long, folk have been adventuring together, knowing the details of one another's lives, striving a little but companioning far more than striving, kindling to one another's interests instead of practicing the faint morality of mere civility.

Zona Gale,
Friendship Village Love Stories, 1909.

The editorial policy [of *Small Town*] reflects a belief that small countryside communities, built to human scale by the people who live there, are ultimately the places which will survive the growing problems which mega-culture has imposed on our lives in this century. Many volumes of social science research suggest that it is largely in the countryside where small towns, family farms, small businesses, and local government can contribute to a sense of community. It is here, in small towns, where the energy and enthusiasm of the young, and the tempered wisdom of older generations, can come to develop common interests.

Editorial page,
Small Town, 1975.

At the turn of the twentieth century, the majority of Americans still lived in small-town and rural communities. Small-town residents saw themselves as quintessential Americans, and with considerable pride and assurance, they proclaimed that the small town was the premiere form of community (Meinig, 1979). As historian Page Smith (1966) notes, town folk believed the town was the place where neighborliness, equality, thrift, frugality, and loyalty were most fully developed. As for cities, town apologists argued that the intimacy, neighborliness, friendship, and democracy of the town were necessarily lost in cities, where "crime, vice, impersonality, unfriendliness, lack of generosity, and the extremes of wealth and poverty" were seen as the norm (Strauss, 1961). The town's social and ideological dominance manifested themselves in the popular literature of the turn of the century. Small towns provided the settings for most novels and short stories, and, in most cases, popular works of the period—like those of Zona Gale—presented an idealized image of the town as the embodiment of community.[10]

Such social and ideological dominance was not to last. Even during the closing decades of the nineteenth century, the industrial city—with its expanding economic and political power and rapidly growing population—clearly signaled the shifting fortunes of the town. By 1920, the United States Census reported for the first time that more Americans lived in urban rather than rural communities. Significantly, this decade also saw the emergence of a new literature of the town in which writers like Sinclair Lewis (1920), Sherwood Anderson (1960), and Edgar Lee Masters (1915) depicted the provincialism, materialism, and limits of the rural community from an increasingly urbane and critical perspective.[11]

By mid-century, the small town had become a marginal form of community in a society dominated by metropolitan cities and suburban satellites. Arthur Vidich and Joseph Bensman (1960) argued that demographic, economic, political decline rendered the town weak and dependent in urban, mass society—a community that "lacks the power to control the institutions that regulate and determine its existence" (cf. Martindale and Hanson, 1969). Grace Metalious, in one of the best selling books of the 1950s, portrayed the town as *Peyton Place*, a New England community that had been corrupted by violence and sex like more urban places, leaving only a veneer of respectability.[12]

Despite such shifting fortunes, the town remained an important cultural symbol. Opening Disneyland in 1955, Walt Disney made turn-of-the-century Main Street the focal point and entryway to his world of fantasy, noting that "Main Street is everyone's home town—the heartline of America."[13] And in small-town America, the ideology of the town also lived on. Despite dependence on the economic and political forces of the larger society, small-town residents still *believed in the town.* Like earlier small-town people, residents of Vidich and Bensman's Springdale proclaimed the town a locus of community, where friendliness, neighborliness, honesty, a commitment to family and religious life, and a belief in equality were still the order of the day.

In Valleytown, Villagers continue to conceive of the town through the perspective of small-town ideology. To Villagers, small towns are the best form of community: natural, quiet, safe, friendly, neighborly, good for families and children. Cities, in contrast, are dirty, crowded, noisy, dangerous, unfriendly, uncaring, and entirely unsuited to—if not actually destructive of—family life. Suburbs provide no rival to the town because the traditional ideology of the town scarcely grants the existence of suburbia, let alone recognizes their claims. Within this perspective on the community landscape, Villagers are certain that small towns are the best place to live, and they readily give their affections to town and country rather than the city or suburb.

Villagers' characterizations of the town, thus, must be interpreted at two levels. Although contemporary beliefs, their statements draw upon the enduring cultural legacy of small-town ideology. Though personally appropriated, their views are part of a socially shared perspective on the American landscape.

Most importantly, Villagers conceive of the town as a place of *community*. In small towns, Villagers contend that human relations are personal, intimate, concerned—unlike cities, where "no one knows anybody" and people are indifferent to each others' needs. Moreover, towns are seen as places where the ties of traditional groups still matter—where families stick together, where people are more concerned with children, where neighbors are real neighbors, and where townspeople are friends.

Villagers also conceive of the town as a *haven*—a place of escape, specifically from the city, more generally from the "problems of American life" symbolized by the city. Villagers no longer see small-town life as the dominant form of community life in America, but they still claim that it is the best. Where cities are too large, crowded, and artificial, small towns are places where open land, peace and quiet, and nature still remain. If city life is too fast, small towns are a refuge where life is slow and people still "have time for people." Although public order seems precarious in the cities, small towns are an asylum—a place where you can "still walk down the street" without fear of riff-raff and violence.

Finally, Villagers conceive of the town as a *simpler world.* As a haven, small towns are less troublesome than cities— posing "fewer hassles to cope with." As a community, they are more concerned and spirited. But the simplicity of the town goes beyond this: for Villagers small towns remain a simplified version of American life. Where cities are fragmented and ex- clusive, small towns are places in which "everybody knows ev- erybody" and "everybody's invited." Where cities are chaotic places with people "all mixed together," small towns are still ordered and safe. Where city life is too complex, small-town life is still direct, personal, and comprehensible.

Chapter 4

Urban Ideology[1]

> The prejudice against cities is a prejudice
> against liberty. To say, as so many people do,
> that New York is a dark and terrible inferno, is
> to say that they hate and fear the multiplicity of
> both the human face and the human imagina-
> tion.
>
> Lewis H. Lapham,
> "City Lights," *Harpers*, 1976.

Beyond Antiurbanism

Interpretations of American attitudes toward the city typically focus on unfavorable beliefs about urban life. Not without
reason: historically, more Americans have viewed the city with
ambivalence or hostility than with delight; the dominant images of city life in American culture have been antiurban, portraying the city in unsympathetic, even prejudicial terms.[2]
Today, when asked about an ideal type of community in which
to live, fewer Americans volunteer "the city" than actually live
in such places (Zuiches, 1982), and residents of cities are
more likely to be dissatisfied with their community than are
inhabitants of other types of places (Marans and Rodgers,
1975). Yi-Fu Tuan (1974), commenting on the antiurban animus of American culture, writes:

> It has become an unthinking reflex for Americans to see the
> city as the farmer and intellectual see it: Babylon-den of iniq-
> uity, atheistic and un-American, impersonal and destructive.

69

The very importance of American antiurbanism, however,
has obscured the fact that urban enthusiasts, though certainly outnumbered, have been a continuing part of the American experience. From Benjamin Franklin to Jane Jacobs,
civic boosters to I-Love-New Yorkers, some urbanites have extolled their community as "the place" to live.[3] Such favorable
sentiment, moreover, has often extended to a general love of
cities as a way of life. Currently, public-opinion surveys of
community attitudes indicate that one in five Americans believes the city "offers the best place to live," a figure that dou-
bles among urbanites (HUD, 1978). And if a substantial
majority of Americans personally prefer to live in suburban,
small-town, or rural communities, a significant minority do
not. Somewhere between 15 and 25 percent of contemporary
Americans may ideally prefer to live in a large or medium-
sized city; among residents of large cities (250,000 +), such
prourban preferences increase to six out of ten urbanites.[4]

In order to develop a cultural interpretation of urban ideology, this chapter explores the way that some contemporary
urban enthusiasts think about communities. Urban ideology,
as a form of community ideology, is a system of shared beliefs
that uses conceptions of community to describe and explain
reality, and that does so in a way that motivates and legitimates an individual's commitment to cities. As such, it is an
ideational system that mediates people's understanding and
experience of community, providing the Urbanist with an interpretive perspective on the American landscape.

Specifically, I will analyze how Urbanists routinely describe urban, small-town, and suburban life, identifying the
typical ways urban enthusiasts conceive of different types of
places. To Urbanists, cities are exciting, diverse, liberal places
that promote individuality and personal freedom. Small towns,
in contrast, are dull, provincial, traditional, and oppressive;
suburbs are bland, conservative, and personally alienating.
Later in chapters 6 and 7, I will suggest how urban ideology
also mediates the way Urbanists think about urban problems
and, in some cases, construct an identity as a city person.

Urbanists, Reluctant Urbanites, and City Boosters

Urbanists are the popular ideologues of the city—people who believe urban life is superior to other forms of community and who, ideally, prefer to live in cities. Although not all Urbanists reside in cities, they are substantially more likely to live in cities than other places, and they are particularly prevalent in large cities. This concentration of Urbanists in big cities certainly arises in part because urban enthusiasts selectively migrate to America's metropolitan centers, forsaking rural and suburban communities in search of the good life. In all likelihood, however, this concentration of Urbanists is also a product of the cultural urbanity of these places: these large cities—and only these cities—have sufficient population and institutional resources to sustain a vital ideology of city life in a pervasively antiurban culture. Residents of such places, as a result, have greater opportunity than do people elsewhere to learn and adopt the favorable perspective on city life of urban ideology.

Though Urbanists tend to be urbanites, not all city residents are urban enthusiasts. Even in the central city of such a large metropolitan area as San Francisco, a substantial minority of residents interviewed are *Reluctant Urbanites:* people who cite a type of community other than the city as their ideal place to live. It would be a mistake to assume, however, that these Reluctant Urbanites are all strongly antiurban in their beliefs about communities and that they dislike living in San Francisco. Unlike Villagers in Valleytown who routinely designate cities as the worst place to live, most Reluctant Urbanites in fact believe cities are neither the best nor the worst type of place in which to live. When asked how they feel about living in San Francisco, they collectively express a rather wide range of emotions regarding their city and urban life.

Revealing the greatest hesitancy, some Reluctant Urbanites voice considerable ambivalence about residing in San Francisco, reflecting the contradictory "pushes and pulls" of belief, opportunity, and constraint. Like the millions of Americans who historically have migrated to the city in search of work, one contemporary, upper middle-class urbanite, for example, voluntarily sacrifices his desire to live elsewhere for the opportunities and access to employment afforded by the city to him and his spouse:

> I wouldn't encourage anyone to move to San Francisco. The permissiveness of this city, the proliferation of fags; I'm getting sick and tired of it. I would like to move out to a suburb, but I've just started a new job in the city, and my wife works here too, which makes commuting a problem for both of us. My son goes to a good public school; this is a good neighborhood, though you can't see it in a city, it's here. But I would move out tomorrow if my wife's situation would change.

Other strong ambivalences may arise—not from expedient migration to the city—but from the inability to flee a once-loved community. Several elderly, working-class San Franciscans with whom I spoke are trapped in the city: the victims of increasing taxes, changing neighborhoods, and declining personal circumstances. Limited by economic resources and their stage in life, they remain city dwellers with little possibility or expectation of leaving the city. When asked to describe San Francisco, one such elderly gentleman responded with a sense of disenchantment and futility, at once defending the city and recounting its "decline":

> I wouldn't recommend the city now. It's not the fault of the city, but of the people who make the rules here. They're Manhattanizing the city, putting up all these big buildings. They want to make it into an insurance headquarters and a convention center, and it's driving industry out. And the little guy pays all the taxes.
>
> And there's muggings and all that, but you can't blame the people. Unemployment has a lot to do with that. And dope. It used to be better. You could go downtown and park your car, and you wouldn't have to leave your money home. It was much better.
>
> [How would you feel about leaving San Francisco?]
>
> I wouldn't care to move, not at my age anyhow, and start all over. If I were younger, I'd probably move. Now, I'd rather be here if they don't ruin the whole town.

Other Reluctant Urbanites, although reporting that they would ideally prefer to live in a place other than a city, clearly enjoy living in San Francisco and—in some cases—even express limited commitments to urban life in general. For example, some young, single, middle-class San Franciscans, particularly those who are relative newcomers to city life, might well be called *Temporary Urbanists*. Though not voicing the unwavering belief in the city of the Urbanist, they may propose that cities are excellent places to live periodically:

> The pace is faster in the city and there's fumes. There are a lot of lonely people, compared to the country, and the people are not as friendly. But there's more to do. It's a neat thing to do for a while. I have to be in a place at a certain time. If I need stimulation, I move to the city. If I need rest, I move to the country.

. . . or at a particular stage in life:

> Where I'd like to live has to be a qualified answer. Without children, it would definitely be a city, like I'm living in now. If I had children it would be a suburb or a small town—and preferably a "suburbury" small town. Something that would be commutable to a place of business, yet where your children can grow up, where they can appreciate being outside. I want to have my cake and eat it, too. While I don't have children, I'm very happy to live in the city and have access to the countryside. If I had children, I would want to live close enough to the city so that we could enjoy the outdoors but also bring the children to the city to learn to appreciate the finer things in life, in addition to cows and horses.

Some such Reluctant Urbanites may well be in the process of becoming Urbanists, discarding their former conceptions of city life and forming new attachments to their city and city life:

> I've thought about where I'd like to live a lot, and I've come to the conclusion that I'd like to live in San Francisco. I've had opportunities to leave, but I just feel very comfortable here. I like the neighborhood stores. San Francisco has neighborhoods. I never expected to find a neighborhood in a city. It's just a nice city. The buildings aren't real tall, there are not the concrete canyons, the feelings you have in another large city.

Moreover, many Reluctant Urbanites are certainly *City Boosters*, if not Urbanists, arguing that *their city* is a "good city," even if cities "in general" are "bad places to live." Such city boosting may well be common among urbanites. Opinion surveys, for instance, indicate that six out of ten urbanites are "satisfied" or "completely satisfied" with the community in which they live, though only a minority of urbanites ideally prefer to live in cities.[5]

This paradox—that American city residents are likely to be a booster of their community but not of cities and urban life in general—may well be encouraged by the general antiurbanism of American culture. Unlike the Villager, who easily identifies his or her community as a typical—and ideal—small town, some urbanites who like the city in which they live may come to believe their experiences are unusual and their city, atypical, because "everybody knows" that "cities are bad places to live." Like the following working-class booster in San Francisco, they dissociate their city from other cities, even denying their "good city" is "really a city":

> Well, you know, I wouldn't call San Francisco a city. Because most of the white-collar workers—those that work in the financial district and live in the suburbs—they don't have far to travel. They come and do their work, and they're happy because they're close to home and there isn't that fast pace and it isn't so congested. They enjoy coming to the city. And the people who live in the city and work around the city do, too. I think people who work in New York only work for the money. I don't think they can stand the cities they live in—Chicago, Detroit, all those. But everybody likes it here.

Urbanists, however, voice few of the ambivalences, reservations, or contradictions of the Reluctant Urbanite. As ideologues of the city, these urban enthusiasts have a relatively strong and integrated sense of cities and urban life. They frequently display a refined knowledge of differences among cities; yet, at the same time, they believe cities, compared with suburbs and towns, provide a relatively distinct and favorable way of life. Although they do not express identical views of community life, they routinely describe places through the interpretive perspective of urban ideology. This perspective—its shared imagery and structure—can be revealed by examining how Urbanists characterize urban, suburban, and small-town life.

The Interpretive Perspective of Urban Ideology

> How do I feel about cities in general? I love 'em!
> Yeh, they're exciting, there's stores, there are
> things to do. Warm!
>
> An Urbanist in San Francisco

The City of Light

> I'm a city person: it's an appreciation for the hu-
> man environment of the urban area. For the
> kinds of choices, all the different kinds of peo-
> ple, the kinds of things that people can get to-
> gether and do, the wild things that go on here
> [laughs], the fun to be had. That's the main
> thing—the human environment.
>
> An Urbanist in San Francisco

The meaning that urban life has for Urbanists can best be conveyed by first looking in some detail at the way that one Urbanist, whom I call Tom Clark, describes the city in which he lives, San Francisco. Though his views are unique in personal detail, they illustrate the imagery and the sense of place of urban ideology.

Mr. Clark is a well-educated, single, middle–aged, professional. He lives in a well-maintained apartment building in an upper middle-class neighborhood of San Francisco. His apartment, which is decorated with American antiques and original prints, reflects his personal interest in the arts. From his living room, Mr. Clark looks out over the city, across San Francisco Bay to the Marin headlands.

Mr. Clark, the youngest child in a large family, was born and raised in a small, eastern city. This community, he believes, was a good place for a child, but, as he grew older, he became increasingly dissatisfied with his childhood home:

> The things I needed as a child were there, but as I grew older,
> I began to feel the need for something more. Art is a big part
> of my life. We were very limited in that town. Once I went to
> New York, I realized there were lots of things that were out
> there. . . . In the fifties, I decided to leave home for San Fran-

cisco, mostly because I felt smothered by my family, they thinking they were doing the right thing for me, but me, not being able to be me, Tom. So out of the top of my head, I said, "San Francisco sounds good." I was twenty-one: you take on quite a bit at that age.

Like other Urbanists, Mr. Clark describes himself both as a city person and a San Franciscan. Early in our conversation he volunteered:

I'm a city boy. I drive 25 miles each way to work. I'm the only one where I work who does this—no one else lives in the city and commutes to the suburbs. I live in the city because it has everything I need and want. Because of the things a metropolitan city offers—what I need to feed my soul.

Though admitting he may leave San Francisco some day, Mr. Clark identifies with the city strongly:

I think until my dying day I'll still have my roots in San Francisco. I'm pretty strongly planted. I'm not saying I will live here 'til my dying day, but I'd still read about it, know about it, and come back to it.

What I feel is unique about San Francsico—and I feel you should have this feeling about any city—is that I feel the city belongs to me: that it's mine. I know there are 800,000 or 700,000 other people out there, but when I wake up and look out in the morning, I say, "Hey, that's me, that's mine." And I feel you should have that kind of feeling about anything you love, whether it's a city, a person, an activity, whatever. And you know damn well it's not yours, but you have this feeling—you identify, you belong to it, you feel it, you're in harmony with it: it's a good feeling that comes over you.

When asked how he would describe San Francisco to someone who did not know the city, Mr. Clark, like other Urbanists, responded enthusiastically to the question:

San Francisco is one of the most cosmopolitan cities in the world. I haven't seen all the cities of the world, but I have seen a good cross section of Europe and parts of the Far East. From the standpoint of a cosmopolitan feeling, it has a very sophisticated type of person who lives here. Not everyone who lives here is sophisticated, but you can find enough of your own kind to feel comfortable no matter what your preferences are relative to music, jobs, travel, sex, whatever. If it's not happening here, it's not happening anywhere. I know we've heard that statement about New York, but I think we can say that truthfully about San Francisco.

From the standpoint of cultural things, I think it's the epitome of any city. We have the number two opera company, and our symphony is number six in the United States—pretty good for beginners. We have a good community, which supports the arts. A fine Jewish community, and we have ethnic and regional people who've come here and made this one of the most glorious cities in the world.

Sitting in my room, looking out the window, I can tell you another reason it's the greatest. Where can you get that kind of view? The Golden Gate, Alcatraz? Aesthetically, it's one of the finest cities.

Job opportunities—I'm not much of an authority on that, but I think there are a good cross section of jobs. I'm not saying there's always a job here for you. And social welfare—I think people try to take care of the problems which come up in the city. Most people the world over know that San Franciscans, if they don't like something, they're the first to get out on the street and say, "Hey, look!" and do something about it. They say there are a lot of radical people here. That's good—we need radical people and conservative people to keep us in check. Basically, though, this is a strong, Democratic, union-type town. They've won their rights with blood, sweat, and tears.

Mr. Clark's description of San Francisco and his relation to the city are instructive because they incorporate many of the central conceptions of city life of urban ideology. Three sets of images are salient to the ideology and are often used by Urbanists.

First, the city is presented as a place of incredible *diversity,* a diversity that is both valued in its own right and that is thought of as a source of *opportunity and excitement.* This view of the city—of its variety and tremendous potential—is offered in various forms by different Urbanists, depending on their specific background and concerns. But the city is always regarded as "the place," where "everything is happening" and where life is rich and enjoyable.

Most often, Urbanists cite the diversity of activities offered by urban life, particularly those centered in entertainment or the arts. For Mr. Clark, the range of opportunities in the serious arts captures center stage. For an elderly, working-class woman, such opportunities provide a backdrop to more mundane possibilities offered by the abundance of organizations in the city:

> In San Francisco there's a variety of things you can do. You need never be lonely. There are very many clubs and all kinds of churches and organizations in connection with the churches. The museums are good, and the theaters, and if you like, you can go to the opera and concerts.

To a young, middle-class woman, the excitement and potential of the city extend beyond play to work:

> San Francisco is a lot faster paced than the suburb, though it's far from New York. It's a different type of living. There are lots of good places to party, there's a good park, and you can go over to Marin. There's a great social life in the city. There's also a lot of competition as far as business goes, but if you've got anything on the ball, you can probably get a better job. They're anxious to promote women. There's just more opportunity.

Urbanists are also likely to portray the city in terms of its diversity of residents. Thus, although they will contrast city dwellers with suburbanites and small-town people, they are also likely to emphasize that city residents are not an urban mass but a variegated lot:

> It's hard to describe city people—there's such a transient population. There's a lot of people [in San Francisco] to seek their fortune from the Midwest. They're here for a reason: women to find men, to get away from the family, etc. The native people, they're hard to characterize because there's such a mix of people. Some are stuck here 'cause they can't get out. The Pacific Heights people, they've got the bucks so it doesn't matter. And we get a lot of gay people here because it's such a liberal city. Who you sleep with, what could I care. Out in the Richmond district, those people just love it and they're your basic working-middle-class person.

This diverse population, moreover, like that of activity, is conceived of as an urban resource, providing enrichment and enjoyment:

> San Francisco has an incredible variety of population. There's really a lot of very [wonderfully] strange people all over the city. There are not any "normal" people in the city, as near as I can tell [chuckles]. The ethnicity of the city, and the availability of a wide variety of goods of all kinds. And all the cultural alternatives—both in the regular and the alternative culture trips. They're all happening here in incredible profusion. That's been a real delight.

Finally, some Urbanists present the city in terms of a diversity of neighborhoods. To a large extent, this view of cities—that they are composed of a mosaic of different areas and communities—parallels an awareness of the diversity of people in the city. To a working-class Urbanist the task of describing San Francisco is equivalent to cataloging the different groups of people living in different sections of the city:

> Well, first of all, San Francisco is a mixture of nationalities. There are certain areas that are predominantly of one type: Filipino, Spanish, Italian. The Germans, Italians, and Swedes—those that were here before—are not as segregated as they used to be. Below Mission Street, it's nearly all Spanish and a lot of Italians. Over the hill they say they have the greatest gay community in the city. They're no problem to me. I've never found one of them that wasn't very polite.

Like the variety of activities and people, neighborhoods are thought to enrich life. For a middle-class Urbanist, exploring neighborhoods is, itself, an enjoyable urban activity:

> You have a good mix of people here in San Francisco. The different backgrounds are still pronounced—not as much as they once were, but you can go to different parts of the city and enjoy different cultures and different atmospheres. The most obvious are North Beach [Italian] and China Town, but you can also go out to Clement Street and enjoy the old Russian restaurants and bakeries. People have found a place to live where they can all get along together and give to each other, to varying degrees of course.

Neighborhoods may even be thought to expand opportunities for different styles of living:

> It isn't hard to describe San Francisco because it's so small and it isn't a city—it's about ten cities in one. Each district is like a city in itself. You have the financial district, which is the most like New York. It's fast and everything goes in a hurry and there's different people. You have your residential areas like this, and you have your gay area, which is apart from every other area. This is mostly an Irish and Italian area. It's been that way for fifteen years now. Spanish and Arabs, they're moving in. You can move to each district and find a different kind of culture. And you have your choice of where you want to live or how you want to live, and nobody gets on your case.

Second, Urbanists present the city as a *liberal place, where people are aware, open-minded, and particularly tolerant* of social diversity. In San Francisco, such urban civility may be mentioned in the context of tolerance of different ethnic and racial groups, but it is the city's gay community—its openness and relative acceptance—that most often draws comment, even by those not entirely pleased by the situation:

> San Francisco's a bright and airy city. There's one thing that's really different about it: there's such a liberal, open attitude with regard to a lot of things. In this neighborhood, the gays walk up and down the street all the time. I'm accustomed to it, but it still affronts me. But I realize it's an existence that is facilitated in the city that is a maze of these subcultures that are along Polk Street or up in Noe Valley. They seem to get along so well. San Francisco has that to offer. Even if I don't appreciate it all the time, I see it as a good thing.

Though Urbanists in San Francisco propose that such civility[6] is particularly developed in their city, they also believe that urban life generally produces openness toward others:

> You get a broader perspective in the city—that you wouldn't get in a small town. It's more multiracial, more international.

You'd have to learn to be a bit more tolerant than you have to be in a small town.

Finally, Urbanists present the city as a place that enhances *personal freedom*. This image of urban life is, of course, closely related to those images of the city as a place of diversity and liberality. Because of the diversity of people in the city, cities are places where, in the words of Mr. Clark, you can "find your own kind." To another Urbanist, these opportunities for personal choice are the basis of a happier life in the city:

> The city can be so many things to so many different people. There are so many different lifestyles, so many different ways of living in this small, little city. I lived in the suburbs of southern California, and it was monotonous. It was very, very homogeneous. Here, there are different races, languages, all kinds of religions, groups, everything. So I think a person could have an easier time finding happiness in San Francisco because you find people that you identify with more readily than in some other place.

Urbanists also describe cities as places of personal freedom by proposing that city life protects personal privacy. Cities, thus, for Mr. Clark, are a place to "get away from the family." For others, they are described as places where one's personal life is not subject to the scrutiny and criticism of neighbors. This view of cities, as we shall see, is typically voiced by Urbanists when criticizing the lack of privacy in small-town and suburban life. The following Urbanist, however, who currently lives in a suburb, directly portrays the city as a place where the privacy of the individual is respected:

> City people are really something. I get all tripped out on city people. They are kick-back-and-watch-what's-happening sort of people. They aren't too involved—well, they are involved, but they don't push themselves on anybody. They kept pretty much to themselves unless you asked for something. Then they were more than helpful. If you want something, it's there, but the people aren't after you all the time. It's not the same with a small town—you have no choice.

The Provincial Town

> I've never lived in a small town. I've only read about them and
> I know some people who come from them. If I had to live
> in one, I know I'd die—not physically, but emotionally and
> mentally.

Although the central images of urban ideology are those
that characterize cities and urban life, urban ideology also
provides basic images of the small town. These images are often critical of town life, and they help define the virtues of
modern urban life by providing a contrasting place that lacks
urban virtues. Like Villagers, whose use of small-town ideology makes them antiurban, Urbanists, drawing on the unfavorable imagery of small-town life, are often small-town critics.

Before examining these critical images of small-town life,
it is worth noting briefly two other aspects of the way Urbanists think about small towns. First, though most individuals
in this study use the term "small town" to designate relatively
small communities, numbering perhaps in the thousands, Urbanists sometimes refer to places of considerably larger size
as "small towns"—places like Eugene, Oregon (82,000) and
Champaign, Illinois (62,000). Contrary to a few Villagers in
Valleytown who fear that their community, nearing 10,000,
is rapidly becoming a "city," Urbanists, with their strong commitments to urban life, transform small cities into small
towns.

Second, not all Urbanists are small-town critics. Some,
like the following lifelong resident of cities, simply reject the
urban portrayal of the town, and, lacking other imagery or experience with the town, they refuse to characterize town life:

> I can't really say about small towns 'cause I haven't lived in a
> small town. You know [laughs] about all I can say is from
> passing through or spending a bit of a summer. My only real
> contrast is from one city to another: I've been a completely
> urbanized person. You know [laughs] if an earthquake came
> or a nuclear war or something, and we survived, I couldn't
> live on a farm. I'm just urbanized.

Others, as we shall see momentarily, use the urban portrayal of the suburb to provide defining contrasts to city life

and may regard the small town as a marginal place, even granting it some virtues. This lack of sharp identity for the town among some Urbanists indicates that the town—particularly the rural small town—is becoming increasingly peripheral to the experience and consciousness of some Urbanists.

Despite this tentativeness among a few Urbanists, urban ideology provides a strong, critical, contrasting view of the town so that many Urbanists—and *only* Urbanists—hold highly critical views of small-town America. These urban critics of the town often begin describing the town by calling it *provincial.* Small towns, they argue, are "cut off" from contemporary American life, particularly from the cultural and recreational opportunities of urban life. Thus, a young, married, professional man in San Francisco comments:

> Small towns tend to be provincial, closed-minded, lacking in availability of a selection of material wants, of diverse cultural activities, and of opportunities for growth in relation to the finer things of life. How's a kid from a small town in Iowa going to learn to enjoy a good French restaurant or the symphony?

For a working-class woman of San Francisco, the "finer things of life" are different, but the theme is the same:

> A small town, hum. It wouldn't be that great. Not much to do—it would be boring. You'd have to travel too far to enjoy anything, to the big city you're nearest, to see the theater, or baseball, or football—anything except maybe roller derby. Also, you'd have to do a lot of driving to get your shopping done.

Moreover, small towns are provincial because "they're behind the times." A young middle-class Urbanist, presently living in Bayside, describes her reaction to living in a country town:

> I'm not accustomed to a small town. It was culture shock to move to that type of place, that's what it was. I couldn't believe it: the women were still running around with Mamie Eisenhower hairdos. Incredible!

An Urbanist of Bayside, who admires some qualities of the town, notes:

> I think cultural changes lag a bit in small towns because of the general conservatism, not ideologically, but just a general resistance to change. There are a lot of things about a small town that make you think it's 1965. Little things, like teenagers still cruise, just like it was in Findlay, Ohio, in 1965. The negative side of that is equally true, as far as racial interaction. I imagine it's going to take a longer time to settle down in a small town.

Critics of the town also characterize small-town life as *traditional.* Like the man just quoted, they may point to the general conservatism of the town. When politics arise, these critics typically suggest that small towns are not only conservative but too conservative:

> Small-town people are mostly conservative. I think they are a little out of touch with the whole society. And I don't think you'll get your political reformers from small towns. You're more likely to get your extremists and conservatives, your right-wingers, from small towns.

The traditionalism of the town is also attributed to small-town people. To a young, middle-class woman in San Francisco, small-town people are less creative and open:

> Small-town people are probably not as imaginative or adventuresome as city people. They're not as interested in developing—more just getting on with things.

To a retired, working-class Urbanist, small-town people lack the vision and motivation "to get ahead":

> I had a friend in the Army. He came from a small town in Oklahoma. He couldn't read nor write. He said, "My old man didn't have to read and write. Why should I have to read and write? He's doing all right." In a small town, if your father was a farmer, they expect your kids to be a farmer. In other words, if it was good enough for your father, it's . . . my father was a teamster. It was never good enough for me, and he never tried to hold me back.

Finally, critics of the town usually characterize the town as *personally oppressive.* This image of the town may arise as a personal reaction to the provincial and traditional character of town life:

> I've lived in two places I call small towns. . . . To me, under 30,000 is not manageable for my lifestyle. It's very boring— not enough to do—like there's no restaurants and the shopping is expensive. Usually, small-town people have not traveled as much, and they have a narrower range of interests. I found it very confining, socially and otherwise. They seemed secure and happy with their lot. They didn't feel the restlessness I did. I actually felt trapped at times. I wanted to get on a freeway or see an airport, to get out of there.

The image is frequently suggested through an attack on the sociability of the town. "Small-town life," they argue, "is like living in a goldfish bowl." And the sociability of the town is symptomatic, not of friendliness, but of boredom and pettiness:

> Small-town people are too god-damn neighborly! I told you I don't like all my neighbors over when I come home. I don't mind lending people things, but the cups of coffee—dum, de dum, de dum. It isn't the monetary thing, 'cause they always return it. But it's just an excuse to get into your house. They check to see how things are. They're too petty for me. And they're only interested in their own little world. They aren't interested in the world as itself.

Lastly, the oppressiveness of the town may be described as an assault on personal autonomy and individuality; overtly by intolerance:

> Small towns are purgatory to me. I almost invited the breakup of my marriage to get out of a small town. The main thing is the red-neck people. They're narrow-minded, very judgmental. If you're a bit different, you're strange to them. It's just mainly the people.

> . . . covertly by conformity:

> I get the impression that small towns are really dull and that I would be bored stiff. There would be this tightening by the community around me—in my subconscious—about what I could do, how I could dress, and I think that would take effect, as well as being bored.

The Vanilla Suburb

> There isn't a sense of community if you live in a
> suburb, where if you live in a small town or a
> city, at least you've got something you feel you
> belong to. I don't think there's an identity to a
> suburb. When you say suburb, people just have
> this picture of semiurban areas all across the
> country and they're all the same. Small towns
> have taste, big towns have taste, and they
> vary from one to another. But suburbs are all
> the   same—it's   vanilla   whether   it's   East
> coast or West.
>
> An Urbanist

Suburbs, as a type of place, and suburbia, as a way of life,
provide the third and final element of the place landscape of
urban ideology. As with small-town imagery, the imagery of
suburbia is defined through its relation to urban life, and it is
difficult to understand the unfavorable portrayal that Urbanists often give suburbia unless their views are seen in the context of their beliefs about cities.

It is also true, however, that suburbs may be defined in
relation to beliefs about small towns. In some cases, Urbanists
portray the suburb as a midpoint along a rural-urban contin-
uum: suburbs are then thought moderately good places—less
provincial, traditional, and oppressive than small towns but
not as exciting, diverse, liberal, or liberating as cities. In other
cases, Urbanists are sharp critics of suburbia, arguing that
suburbs are "as bad" or "even worse" than small towns. They
may even contend that suburbs combine the "worst of both
worlds," joining less desirable features of city life to the inad-
equacies of the town.

To the Urbanist critic of suburbia, the most significant defining characteristic of suburbia is its sameness. Unlike cities, with their particularity and their internal diversity of
activity and people, suburbs are presented as uniform and homogeneous. Thus, for example, an Urbanist may suggest that
suburbs, as peripheral and dependent places, lack sufficient
autonomy "to be" distinct places:

> Suburbs are not as provincial as small towns, but they lack
> an identification of—what's the word—of urban character.

They're pretty much gray areas, pretty much bedroom communities. As such, people cannot identify with the city in which they work, but they can't develop a sense of civic pride about where they live either.

More often, suburban life is said to be uniform, and suburban people are described as excessively homogeneous. To a young Urbanist reluctantly living in a suburb with her children, suburbs are identical—and dominated by housewives:

I lived in a suburb in Germany and here, and suburbia is the same in every country. What you're stuck with is your typical, little housewife with nothing to talk about except the butter going up three cents. A housewife and a station wagon hauling kids around. They have a very shallow existence. They have nothing to do but watch the next-door neighbor and see if they got a new, bigger station wagon. It's very much like small-town people, but their men have different jobs.

To an Urbanist in San Francisco, suburbs are interchangeable and inhabited by mobile businessmen:

There's sort of a Gypsy mentality in America—so many people moving. The people I've met working for corporations who move often live in suburbs. These people, the corporate Gypsies, they have this unity of culture. They move into suburban Cleveland and the next month to suburban Los Angeles, but they're in the same place. Their heads are in the same place and they choose places that are all alike. That would be the most homogeneous element of American life— the suburban, as opposed to the little town or the big city.

In the most vitriolic portrayal of suburbia, Urbanists contend that the uniformity of suburban life and people is a product of the suburb. Here, the physical uniformity of the suburb is thought to produce and sustain uniformity in suburban life:

When I think of a suburb, I just have this vision of these little, wooden people who are turned out at a factory . . . everybody is the same. They have the same ambitions, the same goals. When I lived in that suburb, I didn't feel I was adding a thing to this glob of humanity. You become a part of it, out of habit and boredom.

You see, I don't consider suburbia a town. A town or a
city is a unit—it has all the working parts. I see suburbia as
a piece that doesn't really function on its own. It's very limited and restricted, though maybe that's where I was living.
But it was atrocious. It was like that song. I can't remember
who sang it, the ticky-tacky sort of thing.[7] I was married to a
young-aspiring, and you lived in a duplex, which was one of
many duplexes for five miles and they were identical. And everybody who lived there was a young couple, and they all
worked for the corporation. They were all young wives with
one baby and another in the oven. They have the mother's
brigade: every morning at nine, everybody put their little kid
in a stroller and marched up and down this five-mile block.
And that was routine. And there were coffee klatches.

It just drives me insane when I think about it still. That
was the entire life I remember. Our whole social life revolved
around that sort of activity: bridge at night, all the nice little
yucky things. There's nothing wrong with bridge but when
it's night after night with the same people. Ugh! I felt like a
cog in a machine.

When asked to describe suburbia, Urbanists are also
likely to suggest that suburbs are *boring* places, not simply
because they lack the amenities of urban life, but also because suburban culture lacks the complexity of urban life:

Suburbs are great places for kids, period! They don't hold
nearly the stimulation, the different kinds of things to be interested in, that the city does. The things suburbs offer, including the people who live there, are pretty standard.
There's a junior college that offers the usual courses; the
high schools all look about the same, and they have about
the same quality of education. And everybody drives about
the same kind of car, which is usually a station wagon. And
they have two dogs and two kids. There are very few minorities and very few people other than the middle class. The
prime motive for living there has got to be it's a great place to
raise kids.

Or suburbs, particularly suburban developments, are said
to be dull because they attract dull people:

Life in suburbs is boring. It's tough to pin down but the kind
of people who live in suburbs are the kind of people who bore

me. Maybe it's just the impression I get from tract homes. They're boring: one is virtually the same as the next. But the physical environment would attract the kind of people who live there. There's just not interesting people.

In the same manner that Urbanists contrast the traditionalism of the small town with the liberality of the city, Urbanists also portray suburbs as *conservative* places compared to the city. Like small-town life, suburban homogeneity makes suburbanites less aware of social diversity and, ultimately, *less tolerant* of others:

> I think a lot of suburban people are really less open, less aware of what's going on around them, than city people because they haven't seen as much. They've lived in a protected environment. Like the suburb I visit: it's practically all white, Anglo-Saxon, whatever. Anyone who goes around in that environment is not going to be as accepting.

Urbanists may also suggest, however, that the conservatism of suburbanites is less a product of suburbia than a reason for its very existence. Suburbanites, thus, may be criticized for being "escapists":

> I've found that a lot of people in this suburb and other suburbs I've visited tend to be slightly paranoid. That's why they live there. The type of person with a certain amount of prejudice and apprehension—there's a lot of that in suburbs.

. . . or for being unconcerned about others:

> Suburbs are different from cities. They tend to be kind of free-flowing and not concerned with the rest of the world. They're much more into their own selfish needs. Typically conservative people. Many of the characteristics of small-town mentality are found in a suburb—they're narrow-minded.

In the strongest formulation, suburbs and suburbanites are portrayed as exploiters of cities and urban residents:

> I think suburbs are a social and economic imbalance. It's an attempt by a certain segment of the population to isolate it-

self from everything in the world. It's a parasitic relationship
with the big town. They want all the advantages of a big city;
yet they refuse to contribute to its tax base, even exercising a
certain amount of political power there. I think it's the class
of people who live in suburbs more than suburbs.

Finally, Urbanists may portray suburbs as places of *moral
malaise and personal estrangement*. This imagery of suburbia is less salient than other conceptions, and some Urbanists may at once note its existence and question its veracity.
Others, however, suggest that the uniformity, conservatism,
and ennui of suburban life is associated with—and may
cause—a moral and personal impoverishment. The boredom
of suburban life may be said to support promiscuity:

> Suburbs seem to get into cliques and they do a lot of wife-
> swapping. I know that for a fact. They've got a looser moral
> standard. I wouldn't have any part of their lousy life. You be-
> long to the Elks, you belong to this and that, but I remember
> patting fannies at every New Year's party I went to in the sub-
> urbs. No objections. The wives are bored, and the husbands,
> when they get off work in the city, they go to a hot bar where
> the pick-ups are easy. They didn't get home 'til eight or nine
> in the evening. They were playing. I never had anything
> against that [chuckles], but I couldn't get away with it. They
> got a dull life down there in the suburbs.

Suburban uniformity and privilege may be thought personally stultifying:

> Suburbs—they're the unhappy medium. They're not the city
> and not the country. They have an aura of lethargy that I find
> stifling. They're not the wilderness, but they don't have the
> cultural advantages of the city. And the suburb I know best,
> it's very affluent, so it's just that their values have been
> somewhat warped. Young people, their main concern is Por-
> sches and BMWs. Their conversation doesn't go too far out-
> side that.

Suburban uniformity may encourage competitiveness
and dissatisfaction:

> I'm a bit biased against suburbs, now. They're lacking in
> depth, in lifestyle. It becomes the stereotypical situation
> where you have two cars, the dog, the fenced-in backyard, the

kids, and the above-ground swimming pool. It's the easiest way for people to get into the game of keeping up with the Joneses. And suburban people, they're as unsure as any other people. The divorce rate seems higher there than any other location. There's a general feeling of dissatisfaction.

Even the family life of suburbia may be portrayed as lacking integrity and vitality:

Suburban life is pretty routine, especially for the housewife and the commuters. Lot of puttering around the house. Also there are a lot of children—spoiled children. They find themselves in the suburbs with nothing to do. They're very idle, not like the city where you can go to the movies or downtown. That creates a lot of problems. Because the parents are tired—the father, when he comes home from the commute, the mother from doing housework all day—kids don't get the kind of parental attention that you get in the city.

Perspective and Landscape

When seen as a whole, urban ideology provides a relatively coherent view of the community landscape. This ideological perspective is clearly systemic: beliefs about cities are embedded in beliefs about towns and suburbs. Moreover, the logic of this perspective is less one of fact than of an interpretive framework. In its presentation of city, suburb, and town, urban ideology selectively portrays urban life at the expense of suburban and small-town life. To the Urbanist, viewing places through the structured imagery of the perspective, the city appears inherently superior to suburb and town—the locus of the good life. This image structure is composed of four major contrasting conceptions of community.

First, urban ideology portrays cities as places of the *center*, while suburbs and small towns are viewed as *peripheral places*. Cities are "where it's at": the locus of social life, full of opportunity, exciting. Small towns, in contrast, are provincial, both "out of touch" and "behind the times." Suburbs, if less peripheral spatially and historically, are said to be marginal functionally. They are a social fragment, lacking an identity of their own, dependent on the center for work and play.

Second, urban ideology presents cities as places of *diversity*, while towns and suburbs are portrayed as *simple or uni-*

form. In the ideology of the city, diversity is valued both in its own right and as a source of excitement and personal enrichment. In contrast, small towns are portrayed as not only simple but too simple—limited in opportunities and boring. Suburbs, if not too simple, are too uniform. Juxtaposed to the diversity of the city, suburbs are thought a place of the "mass," where identical houses, standard people, and a monotonous way of life are repeated endlessly.

Third, urban ideology presents cities as *liberal* places, while suburbs and small towns are viewed as *conservative* places. Where urban life is thought to produce expanded awareness of life, personal openness, and a tolerance of social and racial differences, small-town life is portrayed as excessively traditional—over conservative in politics, lacking in personal vision, narrow-minded about matters of race. Like small-town simplicity, suburban uniformity is thought to provide a poor social environment for learning acceptance of people who are different. Moreover, the conservatism of suburbanites may be viewed as self-serving—the stance of those who wish to escape the responsibilities of metropolitan life.

Finally, urban ideology identifies cities with *individuality and personal freedom*. Where cities provide privacy for the individual, small towns *constrain* individuals: they are petty, gossipy, and personally oppressive. Where the diversity of the city supports individuality and personal enrichment, suburban uniformity causes a personal *estrangement* manifested in conformity, competitiveness, and ennui.

Interpreting Urban Imagery

Since the publication of Morton and Lucia White's *The Intellectual versus the City* (1964), investigations of American attitudes toward cities have become more sensitive to the cultural sources of antiurban sentiment. Increasingly, the hostility that many Americans express toward cities has been seen to bear the imprint of an antiurban culture. This antiurbanism, moreover, is not simply, or even primarily, a "reflection" of current conditions in cities, but is the legacy of conflict over the role—and the meaning—of cities in American society. Historical conflicts of rural and urban Americans, of native and immigrant, of Protestant and Catholic, and recently, of white and black Americans, have each contributed to a dominant cultural repertoire of antiurban beliefs. As a result, many contemporary Americans are antiurban not because of the realities of city life, not because of their experiences with cities, but because they have learned to think about cities in ways that fundamentally prejudice their feelings about urban life.

This cultural interpretation of American antiurbanism deepens our understanding of American sentiment toward cities and other communities. The recognition that antiurban sentiment cannot be adequately understood as a simple, direct response to city life helps explain why those Americans with *least* experience with cities are most likely to dislike them. Villagers in Valleytown, drawing on the antiurban beliefs of small-town ideology, routinely express an antipathy for cities that even exceeds that of the Reluctant Urbanites in San Francisco. The general antiurbanism of American culture may also help explain why favorable popular sentiment toward cities among American urbanites has often taken the form of boosterism. Urbanites, "knowing" that cities are "bad places to live," may tend to attribute the virtues of city life to their "atypical, unique city," rather than to an urban way of life. Ultimately, an appreciation of the cultural impact of antiurbanism suggests that many of the problems that contemporary cities face may well be the product, rather than the source, of popular attitudes toward urban life.

However pertinent, this cultural interpretation of American attitudes toward cities has lacked an appreciation of the fact that urban enthusiasts are also part of the American experience and that their sentiments are also culturally mediated. In short, it has lacked an adequate conception of Urbanists and of urban ideology. In this chapter, we have seen that urban ideology, as an interpretive perspective on city, suburb, and town, also mediates the way that urban enthusiasts think and feel about the community landscape. Because urban ideology symbolically portrays cities as the locus of the good life, Urbanists, by adopting the shared perspective of the ideology, simultaneously learn what cities are "really like" and affirm their commitment to urban life. Urbanists believe cities are the good community: a place of remarkable diversity, exciting, bursting with activities, open and tolerant, a source of freedom and individual fulfillment. Conversely, Urbanists

think small towns are provincial, behind-the-times, traditional, and personally oppressive; suburbs, too homogeneous
and uniform, boring, conservative, and personally alienating.
Unlike those Americans who see the city as a "Babylon-den of
iniquity, atheistic and un-American, impersonal and destructive," Urbanists know cities make the good life possible.

Chapter 5

Suburban Ideology

> Suburbs, like all community forms, have the
> power to arouse emotion and partisanship. As
> new community forms arise, they become in-
> vested with symbolic meaning and enter the
> arena of public opinion.
>
> Sylvia F. Fava,
> "The Pop Sociology of Suburbs and New
> Towns," 1973.

Suburbia: Nightmare or Dream?

Few transformations of the American landscape have been
as dramatic as post–World War II mass suburbanization. Although suburban expansion predates this period by half a
century, the rate and scale of suburban development in the
years following the war increased dramatically, supported by
an expanding economy, strong demand for new housing, government housing and transportation policies that favored suburban growth, and the flight of white Americans from the
growing presence of black Americans in the central city. In
1930, two out of three Americans living in a metropolitan area
resided in the central city rather than the suburban ring. By
1970 the majority of metropolitan residents were now suburbanites and, for the first time in American history, more
people lived in suburbs than in either central cities or nonmetropolitan areas.[1]

Popular commentators and social scientists greeted the
dramatic arrival of the suburbs in the 1950s with equally spirited debate about the nature of suburbs and suburban life. To

the extent that suburbs had received notice earlier in the century, they had been viewed favorably. From the streetcar suburbs of the turn-of-the-century industrial city to the greenbelt communities of the 1930s, suburbs were advanced as a healthy alternative to the physical, social, and moral dangers of the city.[2] Suburbs continued to have their defenders in the 1950s, who identified suburbia with the American dream: the new locus of the American way of life. Yet, for many commentators, suburbs—and the way of life they supposedly engendered—posed a serious threat to the vitality of American society. In *The Organization Man* (1957), the most famous of such exposés, William Whyte charged that suburbs were places of not only physical but social conformity, accompanied by extreme transience, a hyperactive social life, growing conservatism, and status anxiety over the competitiveness of middle-class life.

In reaction to this highly critical interpretation of suburbia, scholars studying suburbia in the 1960s argued that the belief that suburbia was creating a new and deleterious way of life was a myth, unsupported by social research on these communities. Sociologists such as William Dobriner (1963), Bennett Berger (1960), and Herbert Gans (1967) demonstrated that suburban communities differed significantly in social class and historical origins, that many of their purported ills were nonexistent, and that other elements of suburban life were better understood in terms of the class- and family-status of their inhabitants than the suburban context of the community.

Because the critical view of suburban life appeared as erroneous as it was popular, scholars of American culture and suburbia proposed various explanations for the myth's acceptance. Scott Donaldson (1969) contended that the attack on suburbia was symptomatic of the continuing strength of American pastoralism. Commentators who unrealistically expected suburbia to bring about a "return to nature, a return to the small village, a return to self-reliant individualism" were necessarily disappointed with the reality of suburbanization and, as a result, were unreasonably critical of suburban life. Bennett Berger (1960) argued that the popularity of this oversimplified view of suburbia expressed the fundamental ambivalence of Americans toward social diversity. Here, the accentuation of suburban, middle-class uniformity represented the most recent ideological attempt to render Americans homogeneous, despite the continuing class, racial, and ethnic diversity of American society. Finally, other writers proposed that the attack on suburbia, like that on the town thirty years earlier, simply represented a condemnation of American middle-class life and values, so readily visible in and symbolized by the suburban landscape (Dobriner, 1963; Fava, 1973; Wrong, 1972).

Although popular interest in suburbia has waned in recent years, public criticism of suburbia may again be on the rise. Beginning with the release of the President's Task Force on Suburban Problems in 1968, suburbs have again been portrayed as places beset by social problems (Haar, 1972). Now, however, such problems are not linked to the nature of suburban community but rather to the "urbanization of the suburbs." Suburbs are portrayed as facing those problems traditionally associated with city life, particularly crime, poverty, high tax rates, and failing school systems (Schwartz, 1976).

Despite the considerable attention given to the interpretation of both suburban life and imagery, few scholars have examined how Americans actually think and feel about suburbs and suburban life, nor has much attention been given to how suburban residents interpret the meaning of their suburban experience. Perhaps such research has been deemed unnecessary: irrespective of the public debate over suburban life, Americans have seemed to demonstrate a clear and highly favorable conception of suburbia through their migration to the suburbs.

Yet some research suggests that this assumption may be problematic. For example, studies of community preferences indicate that a somewhat smaller proportion of Americans say they ideally prefer to live in suburbs than currently live in them. This apparent anomaly is explained in part by the fact that many Americans who want to live in small communities adjacent to cities think of such places as small towns, not suburbs (Zuiches and Fuguitt, 1972). Such "misclassification" is significant because it suggests that many individuals have little sense of suburbia as a way of life, or, more complexly, that they define suburbs differently than do social scientists and commentators. Similarly, when individuals who have moved to suburbs have been queried about their reasons for the move, they have often focused more on housing characteristics than on community attributes (Gans, 1967). Such a vocabulary of motives is certainly consistent with a strong conception of suburban life, but it may indicate that individuals are not interpreting their actions within the context of a well-defined suburban ideology.

In this chapter I will explore two aspects of popular belief and sentiment about suburbs. First I will argue that suburbs, like cities and towns, do have a community ideology that some individuals, whom I will call *Suburbanists*, appropriate to define a strong and highly favorable sense of suburban life. Although suburban ideology is clearly derivative of urban and small-town ideology in some of its imagery, it portrays suburbia as a distinct way of life, preferable to either city or town. To the Suburbanist, suburbia represents a middle ground—the *"best of both worlds"*—drawing on the virtues of cities and small towns, yet lacking their limitations.

Second, I will also describe how residents of suburbs often diverge in their basic ideological orientation toward suburbia. Depending upon their social class and history of residence, inhabitants of suburban Hillcrest and Bayside may be Suburbanists, Villagers, or Urbanists. As a result, these suburban neighbors differ not only in their conceptions of suburban life but also in their very definition and understanding of the community in which they live.

Suburban Ideology

The Middle Landscape of Suburbia

The sense of place of the suburban ideologue may be illustrated by examining in some detail how one committed Suburbanist, Frank Weber, describes the suburb in which he lives and the community landscape of city, suburb, and town. Mr. Weber, his wife, and two children live in an attractive ranch-style home in upper middle-class Hillcrest. He is in his late thirties, college-educated, and employed in a managerial position at a private corporation. A native Californian, he was raised in another suburb in the San Francisco Bay area. It was, he remarked, a very nice "sort of suburban place":

> No industry, close friendships, very pleasant, no social problems. We played ball and had a good time; left our doors open —the way it used to be, I guess. Very typical—no pressures.

He lived there through college and the early years of his married life; then he and his wife moved to a house in Hillcrest. I asked Mr. Weber why he had moved to Hillcrest:

> There has always been sort of an attraction for Hillcrest for me—it would be sort of a paradise, if you will. When I was a kid, somebody always had an aunt out there, and it would be warm, and there would be swimming pools, and it would be just terrific. It was always in the back of my mind.
>
> It's close enough to the city or working towns and yet still sort of a country atmosphere. And the school systems here are quite good. And to be very honest with you, we didn't want to move into Oakland—there's always that black thing. We didn't want to live next to blacks. I'm not saying that's good or bad.

When asked how he would describe Hillcrest to someone who was not acquainted with the community, Mr. Weber replied:

> Obviously, Hillcrest is a very nice community. The homes are all very nice. You're going to pay more for a home, but you're going to get more out of it. The school system, the weather and, again, you have that insulation, that buffer—that distance from the city. And the people out here—the friends we've met—their likes and dislikes are very similar to ours. We love outdoor activities, play a lot of tennis. . . . You have a tendency to migrate towards people who have the same interests as you do, wherever you go. It's a great place to raise kids. It's clean and the crime rate's relatively low. . . . A few robberies once in a while, but. . . . It's just nice: you can go out and take walks in the evening.

Mr. Weber believes that Hillcrest is a fairly typical suburb, though more well-to-do than most. Suburbs, he notes, have good school systems, are safe places to live, and are "just nice, comfortable, the *way it ought to be*." Mr. Weber's stance toward Hillcrest and suburban life is shaped by his views on cities and small towns. He is strongly antiurban, seeing cities primarily as a locus of problems, and like other Suburbanists, he argues that cities, at best, are "good places to visit":

> There's obviously the faster pace in cities—the intensity of the place, the crime. And I keep referring to my children: I wouldn't want them there. The traffic problems, congestion,

pollution, all the things you read and hear about. Cities drive
me nuts. I like to enjoy them—maybe one evening, or if I've
got something specific to do: going to a play or out to dinner,
that's terrific. But living there on a day-to-day basis . . .
there's not an escape.

Mr. Weber is more sympathetic to small towns; he feels
they may be even more serene and slow-paced than suburbs.
But that serenity, he also believes, is indicative of their
provincialism:

I think living in a small town would be rather boring—more
so than here. In a suburb it's still pretty much a melting
pot—you get people from a lot of different areas and backgrounds, which is stimulating. I don't know who in hell I'd
hang out with if I lived in a small town, or what I'd talk about:
"Gee, the corn's growing great." It would be rather boring.

Mr. Weber's description of Hillcrest and of the community
landscape of city, suburb, and town is instructive because it
incorporates much of the central imagery of suburban ideology. Three sets of imagery of suburbia are salient to the ideology and are frequently volunteered by Suburbanists.

First, Suburbanists often describe suburbs as *clean,
quiet, and natural places.* Although close to the city, suburbs
are still thought to retain these virtues of town and country
life. A Suburbanist in Bayside, for example, identifies suburbia
with the natural landscape:

Well, a suburb: it's close enough to a city for convenience
sake or socializing, but yet it still—you have trees and cows
and all the familiar country sounds. I like nature, natural
things, birds. I like to be able to see the trees on the hill, the
openness, and not being crowded.

And like small towns, suburbs may be portrayed as places
that are easygoing and quiet:

Living in Hillcrest, it's a quiet life. Nothing really happens out
here. You have no big shopping centers, one little theater,
maybe three bars in the whole town, and it's just a quiet residential area. Just one little business strip—I'd like to keep it
that way.

. . . less intense and less formal than cities:

> In general, suburbs are smaller, they're quieter, and the poli-
> tics, for instance, are not as demanding. When you live in a
> city, you always know who the mayor is. Here, I have to stop
> and think who the city manager is. You don't worry about
> such things—it's in the background.

Second, the most salient images used by Suburbanists to
characterize suburbia are those that portray the suburb as a
place of *domesticity.* If small-town ideology proclaims the
town to be the locus community and if urban ideology portrays the city as the place of the individual, suburban ideology
uses *family, home,* and *children* to define the most essential
feature of suburbia and, in doing so, to ennoble and justify
suburban life. At the very least, a Suburbanist will note that
suburbs are places devoted to family life:

> Suburbs—they're close enough yet not too far. Where you
> can get away from the city, where all starting families go. You
> know, tract homes, station wagons, kids. Suburbs serve their
> purpose. They're the place where all young families go before
> moving on.

They are also likely to contend that suburban residents
are particularly interested in matters of home and family life,
and that, as a result, suburban life is especially good for children. Suburbanites, for instance, may be contrasted to city
people, who are thought to be less interested in household activities and staying "at home":

> A real city person likes walking in the city, going to stores,
> shops. They cannot move to a suburb. They don't like to
> drive and they are used to seeing more people. When we
> come from work, we go to the garage, close the garage, and
> come to the house, and our activities are inside the house—
> like personal hobbies. City people like to go out. They don't
> like to water the garden or work on the house. Some people
> in the city don't like to have a house at all.

Suburbanites, conversely, are said to be more concerned
with family life:

I would say our interests in suburbia are very much different from those who live in a city. We tend to probably be more interested in our homes and gardens and our children and with PTA and what-have-you.

... and to be particularly concerned that their children be brought up properly:

The majority of people in a suburb like this are interested in their children, in getting an education for them, that's worthwhile. Also, teaching them some kinds of values.

But Suburbanists contend that the middle ground of suburbia truly distinguishes the suburb as the superior place for raising children. To a working-class Suburbanist in Bayside, the location of suburbs insures access to the city without the dangers of city life:

Suburbs are the best for kids. In a small town you're isolated, where in a suburb you always have access to go up to the big city. It's halfway. You've moved out to a place where you are trying to confine your child, keep them away to a point, where in a small town, you're out completely, isolated from everything.

In a city, a child has less freedom. My kid, he can walk to school, and I don't feel anything is going to happen to him between here and school. If it were just traffic, he'd be as safe there, but the type of person he's likely to run into, it's more dangerous, 'cause they got that many more people.

And in Hillcrest Mr. Weber comments:

In suburbs you get the best of both worlds for raising children. You still have the ease of the lifestyle, the safety, the good school system, and yet you're close enough to the cultural things, if you will, to sort of broaden the education of the children. In a small town you're at a disadvantage. I hate to use the term "country bumpkin," but I think you could easily get taken advantage of if you're from a town once you get out in the real world. . . .

And in the city, there's the congestion—it's unsafe for kids to play. Pollution, the school systems are generally quite poor, only because they have such a melting pot of people that the standards are lowered to cover everyone.

Finally, Suburbanists often emphasize that suburbs, unlike cities, are *safe places*. They may express concern over burglary in the suburbs, but they believe that suburbs offer far greater security to their residents than do cities. This security is valued both in itself and because it is thought essential to other suburban virtues. Because suburbs are safe communities, they are "quiet" places; because they are relatively crime-free, they are excellent for children.

Suburban Views of Town and City

Suburbanists, thus, portray suburbs as quiet, natural, secure places, where life centers on home and family. This sense of suburbia is situated in the context of the middle landscape: a belief that suburbs, as a consequence of their location and size, bring together the best qualities of small towns and cities—without the liabilities of either. This sense of place is based on conceptions of small town and city that are also essential elements in the landscape of suburban ideology.

When Suburbanists describe the small town, they typically portray the town as a good place to live, though not without faults. As a result, they often feel ambivalent about town life, warming to the virtues they attribute to the town, withdrawing from its less desirable features. Suburbanists suggest that small towns, like suburbs, are quiet, natural, and safe places—sometimes proposing that towns surpass suburbs in these qualities. Small towns are thought to be good for children and to have an active community life. If a Suburbanist has formerly lived in a small town, the town's sociability may be recounted in the language of small-town ideology:

> Everybody knows everybody in a small town—that's one thing. There are few strangers in a small town. If somebody was doing something, everybody would know. And it's easier to get from place to place. Everything is within walking distance. There's probably more activities—like Saturday-night dances. It seemed like back home there was a dance every Saturday night.

To the Suburbanist with an urban background, the sociability of the town may be described in a more speculative tone:

> Well, a small town's very hometown. They have strong ties to one another; they're friends through life—at least that's my

image of it. In the town where my wife's parents live, they all
follow the high school football team. And their concerns are
local; they don't go 50 or 100 miles for something. It's a center in itself.

At the same time that Suburbanists extol such features of
town life, they are also likely to suggest that such characteristics of the town also carry liabilities—liabilities not shared by
suburbs. If small towns are attractive for their peace and
quiet, they are suspect for their simplicity:

> I've given it a lot of thought, wondering whether I would ever
> want to move to a small town. I really have mixed emotions.
> On the one hand, I think, "Gee, that would be really nice—
> it's quiet, it's peaceful, you get to know all the people of the
> town," which sounds good to me. But on the other hand, I've
> got a feeling that if I lived there for a year I'd probably get
> bored. Like I say, I have mixed emotions about it.

If small towns provide a sense of community, they also
may be personally confining:

> Small towns? Obviously they're quiet, and everybody knows
> everybody—and probably everybody's business for that mat-
> ter. I feel that's kind of detrimental. Conservative. I'm sure,
> too, that it's much harder for people to break away from small
> towns.

And if small towns provide isolation from the city, they
may also be portrayed as too isolated:

> I've seen small towns in my travels and I've talked with my
> colleagues at work who were born in small towns and farms.
> Life must be very hard for children there. Going to school or
> shopping, they may have to go twenty miles to the nearest
> town, which is really just a bank, a gasoline station, church,
> and so forth. And going to college means going far away. Peo-
> ple from small towns are not able to return to those places.
> They have their parents there, they grew up there, but they
> cannot go back, because they find a more interesting life and
> they never go back.

When Suburbanists describe cities, they are generally anti-urban in orientation and imagery. Some, like Mr. Weber, are highly critical of cities, viewing them exclusively as a locus of pro blems. Others, however, are considerably less vitriolic in their criticisms of city life. Although preferring to live in suburbs, they may, in fact, regard cities as the next best place to live.

The major liabilities of cities are defined by the Suburbanist primarily in terms of the public virtues of suburbs. Where suburbs are clean, quiet, natural, and secure places, cities are polluted, noisy, crowded, artificial, and dangerous. In contrast to the domesticity of suburbanites, city people are thought to be less interested in home and family. At the same time that Suburbanists describe cities in such terms, however, they often note that cities offer cultural and recreational advantages:

> Cities have skyscrapers. The crime is a lot worse than what it would be in a small town because you're more compact, the housing might not be as good, and you don't have enough spreading out areas. Probably your traffic is worse. And the people might not be as friendly, simply because they're pushing and shoving trying to get to and from work. But, of course, naturally, you've got all your activities, like your opera, more arts, museums, more cultural places.

These opportunities may be thought relatively unimportant because suburbanites are "less concerned with such matters." Often these opportunities are said to make cities "good places to visit." And they help to define another advantage of the suburb over either city or small-town life—access to urban amenities without the difficulties of urban life:

> I think people who live in the suburbs feel pretty much the way I do. You still like to go to the city—to have the interaction you have in a city. Yet, you can divorce yourself from it and come out here and live—quote, unquote—"the good life" without being mired down in it on a daily basis.

Suburban Ideology and White Flight

> The reason suburbs have fewer problems than cities is because the type of person who moves to the suburbs is the type who wants something

better. They're the ones who've worked, and they
move to get themselves out of the mainstream
of the city, the traffic, the environment of the
city. They go to work in the city, but this is their
retreat. It's a nice place to live in safety, and
they feel more at ease. It's the type of person
who lives in the suburb who makes it what it is.

If the average person living in those areas of
San Francisco wasn't infiltrated by that kind of
people—robbing, stealing, and so forth—it
would be the same as living in a suburb. The
only reason we have suburbs is that people are
trying to move out and get themselves a little
bit of home life and security. You get enough
people who more or less think alike and have
the same ideas. This is what people try to do.

                                 A Suburbanist in Bayside

There is one image of suburban life that is typically missing from Suburbanists' descriptions of the community landscape and is conspicuous by its absence. In talking about
suburbs and the community in which they live, Suburbanists
do not characterize suburbs as predominantly white communities, despite the fact that the racial segregation of the suburbs is one of the most notable community differences within
the metropolitan context. The 1980 United States census, for
example, reports that nationally 23 percent of the central city
population is black, compared with only 6 percent of the suburban population (Fischer, 1984). This silence not only raises
questions about Suburbanists' conceptions of suburbia but
also about their purported motives for moving to suburbia: social scientists suggest that the rapid growth of the suburbs
has been caused in part by the flight of white Americans from
minorities in the central cities (Gans, 1968).

There are three different ways that this silence might be
understood, and the importance of the topic suggests their
brief review. First, it may well be that some Suburbanists do
not conceive the racial homogeneity of suburbia as distinctly
suburban. For instance, some Americans, including Suburbanists, may recognize racial segregation in housing, but they
may think of it primarily in terms of neighborhoods, rather
than in terms of communities.

Second, it may also be that some Suburbanists, though they recognize urban-suburban differences in racial composition, do not value such differences and thus do not address this community attribute in their generally favorable rendering of suburban life. This possibility receives some indirect support from survey studies of racial prejudice. White residents of metropolitan communities are less likely to be prejudiced against racial minorities than are residents of rural areas, and, in all likelihood, white suburbanites are no more prejudiced than are white urbanites (Greeley and Sheatsley, 1973; Campbell, 1971).

Moreover, studies that investigate why Americans move also report that suburban residents do not comment very frequently on the types of people who live in their community. Suburban residents most often report that they selected their community primarily because of housing, secondarily because of such community attributes as safety, quality of schools, and location to work. In his study of Levittown, New Jersey, for instance, Herbert Gans (1967) found that most people (84%) volunteered that they chose to live in Levittown for house-related reasons. A national survey (HUD, 1978) that directly asked people to rank different reasons for their choice of their community reported similar findings for suburbanites more generally. Three out of four said housing cost, housing quality, and safety were important reasons for moving to their suburb; one in two reported that good schools, work location, and the availability of green, open spaces were important; one in four said that the racial and ethnic background of the people who live in the community was important. And only 3 percent of suburbanites contended that the racial and ethnic background of the people in their community was the first or second most important reason for selecting their suburb.

In light of such findings on racial prejudice and community mobility, Suburbanists may not talk about the racial composition of suburbia simply because they do not place a high value on the racial homogeneity of suburbia. If this were the case, white flight would be a fiction, and the racial segregation of suburbia would simply be the unintended consequence of the search of middle-class whites for better housing, good schools, and green grass in the post–World War II housing market.[3]

Finally, the silence of many Suburbanists on the racial segregation of suburbia may have a quite different signifi-

cance. Some Suburbanists may both recognize and value the
racial segregation of suburbia but may not describe suburbia
in such terms, because they know it is publicly unacceptable
to advance such segregation as a community virtue in contemporary American society. For such Suburbanists, suburban ideology may well provide a socially acceptable way of
talking about suburbia, focusing on housing and domesticity
rather than racial segregation, highlighting peace and security
rather than fear of urban minorities. If so, suburban ideology
would also furnish such Suburbanists with an acceptable vocabulary of motives for white flight from the interracial city to
the confines of suburbia.[4] In this light, survey results that indicate that white suburbanites say they move to suburbia for
housing and green grass cannot be assumed to reflect adequately either their basic conceptions of suburbia or what
they want from suburbia, nor can the racial segregation of
suburbia be seen entirely as the unintended consequence of
white Americans seeking better housing and green grass.[5]

Suburbanists in Bayside and Hillcrest furnish some evidence for this possibility: that Suburbanists use suburban
ideology—either consciously or unconsciously—as a public
mask for racial interests. For instance, no Suburbanist ever
argued that the racial segregation of suburbia was a personal
or social problem, either because such segregation limited the
benefits of social diversity for suburbanites or because it un-
justly limited the opportunities of racial minorities. (Notably,
several Urbanists living in Hillcrest or Bayside did raise such
criticisms of suburbs and their communities.) Moreover, in a
passing remark, some Suburbanists noted that their segregated community had "no racial problem":

> We've really enjoyed living in Hillcrest very much. It's a great
> place to raise children. The weather's great, we love the hot
> summers and the cold winters. And it's quiet, and we have no
> racial problems. We love the hills, too.

Most strikingly, in discussing their reasons for moving to
Hillcrest or Bayside, a few Suburbanists, who had previously
lived in cities, did remark that their move had been, in part,
racially inspired.[6] In moments of candor—"to be honest with
you"—these Suburbanists offered racial motives, providing a

different view of the virtues of suburbia than they had volunteered in their description of suburban life:

> We were improving our circumstances at the time we moved. I hate to say it, but there was the press of minorities in the city. They pushed us a bit. Also, my son was about ready to start school.

Another remarked:

> Some people will not like what I say, but I wasn't used to living with so many different colors of people as when I lived in San Francisco. My decision to move out of San Francisco was because of busing. You can find a good social life in San Francisco, but I am not used to so many colored people and so mixed a city.

For these Suburbanists, at least, suburban ideology provides a socially acceptable imagery for characterizing the contemporary metropolitan landscape, enabling them, for the most part, to avoid discussing the reality of white flight.

Villagers and Urbanists in Suburbia

Suburban ideology clearly endows some residents of suburban Hillcrest and Bayside with a strong, favorable sense of suburbia. These Suburbanists enjoy the particular suburban community in which they live, and they are likely to suggest that their community—Bayside or Hillcrest—is a relatively typical suburb. Suburban ideology, thus, offers Suburbanists a relatively coherent interpretation of the community landscape—one that defines and justifies the belief that suburbs are the best place to live.

Among the residents of Hillcrest and Bayside with whom I spoke, however, Suburbanists constituted a minority of the respondents. This, of course, may be accidental, indicating only that Hillcrest and Bayside are unusual suburbs or that the particular residents I interviewed in these communities are atypical. I believe that this is not the case and that suburban ideology is more often attributed to suburban residents by sociologists and commentators than is warranted. For example, the Northern California Community Study found that only one in five residents of communities in the suburban ring of metropolitan areas ideally preferred to live in a suburb. Moreover, only one in three of these suburban residents even *designated* as a *suburb* the community in which they lived.[7] These nonsuburbanist residents of suburban communities are worth examining because they indicate the diverse ways that suburbanites may think about their communities.

Some residents of Hillcrest and Bayside are best characterized as *Suburban Villagers*. When questioned about their community preferences, they say that they prefer to live in a small town or the countryside. But more significantly, they also think of their community as a small town rather than a suburb, and they typically enjoy living in "their town."

The ideological context in which these Suburban Villagers interpret their sense of place may be of three different types. Several of these people simply have little sense of place whatsoever: their conception of small-town life is usually limited and suburbia has virtually no meaning at all. One such resident of Bayside, for example, could not name any community that she thought was a suburb and, when asked to describe a suburb, replied:

> I don't really know the definition of a suburb—kind of out in the country—a bunch of houses out there. I don't really know.

Other Suburban Villagers—particularly some with rural, working-class backgrounds—are similar to Villagers in Valleytown: they distinguish primarily between cities on the one hand, and town and county on the other. These Suburban Villagers think of Bayside as a small town and use small-town ideology to describe their community's virtues. Although they live in a suburb, an imagery of suburbia is not part of their vocabulary of place.

Finally, some Suburban Villagers have a distinct conception of suburbia, but they do not define "suburbs" as do most social scientists and planners: as communities in the metropolitan context outside the central city. Rather, these people distinguish between suburban communities composed of housing-tract developments, which they call suburbs, and other suburban communities, which they call small towns.

The identification of suburbia exclusively with suburban developments and tract housing usually entails an attribution of suburban ills to such places and, consequently, an exoneration of metropolitan small towns. Thus, one such Suburban Villager in Hillcrest, who thinks of Hillcrest as a small town, describes Hillcrest in the language of small-town ideology:

> Hillcrest is very nice. It's very small. It's beautiful here; there are a lot of trees. All my neighbors love their homes and they're involved in their community. There's a lot of community spirit here because it's so small. You can go to the store and everybody knows you. It's quiet here: the sidewalk rolls up at eight o'clock. It's just the way it should be. The only thing is that freeway out there—I can hear it.

Later, when queried about suburbs, she remarked:

> A suburb was a small town that grew all over. There are housing developments and shopping centers all over the town. The people all live in the same houses. They don't have any identity—they're all the same. They're like a bunch of cattle. They all have the same yard; it's all the same. And they have to drive anywhere they want to go. In this town, there's not a lot of subdivisions—no cheap housing, no rentals, no riff-raff; you don't have to worry about your safety.

It is also worth noting that Suburban Villagers may carry this process of distinguishing between suburban towns and suburban developments one step further, using it to distinguish different neighborhoods—and ways of life—within a single community. In Bayside, a Suburban Villager may call the old core of the community "a small town," while describing the remainder of the community as a suburb. Thus, the following Baysider sees himself as living in a small town, which he believes differs sharply and favorably from the suburban neighborhoods of Bayside:

> When you say Bayside, there are really two Baysides. There's Bayside by the highway, which is subdivisions and housing tracts. Then there's old Bayside. I would be really unhappy over there, but I really like it here [in old Bayside], except that it's a long commute to the city.

> There's a clear distinction between the two areas. The
> suburban part over there tends to be more middle-class, and
> the people in the suburban part of Bayside tend to be more
> like city people: if you walk by on the street you don't ex-
> change greetings to strangers, where down here it's very
> common. Here, in the town, they are older people, more blue-
> collar people, some from the South. But they're very friendly.

In addition to Suburban Villagers, some residents of Hillcrest and Bayside are *Suburban Urbanists*. Although not usually as committed to the city as their counterparts in San
Francisco, these Urbanists believe that cities are good places
to live and, at least conditionally, express a desire to live in a
city. They *all* have previously lived in cities, and, in some
cases, they are socially marginal to their community: younger,
or single parents with children.

Bayside is the home of several Urbanists who are thus reluctant suburbanites. Although most have chosen to live in
Bayside because of the availability of less expensive housing
for families, they would rather live in a more urban community. To one such Urbanist, working-class Bayside is a suburb,
but it is no idyll of family life and security:

> Bayside's not too terribly bad. It's kind of middle income
> here, but we've got a lot of roughnecks. There's a lot of dope:
> this town is crawling with it. And the school's no good—they
> just pass them along.
>
> And so far as culture, there's nothing. Can't go to a show
> out here, there's not plays, museums. We got this lovely li-
> brary a few years ago; before that we didn't have anything.
> And if you don't have a car, you're trapped. There's a lot of
> rednecks out here—hardly anyone with any education. Ex-
> cept for one person across the street, there's hardly anyone
> to communicate with.
>
> No, I don't think it's the greatest place in the world.
> Some people who may move out here think it's great, but to
> me, it's like a rut. I hope I don't have to live here the rest of
> my life.

Upper middle-class Hillcrest is also the home of Urbanists, though their commitment to urban life is relatively weak
and conditional. They believe that Hillcrest is a good place to
live, and they feel that suburbs facilitate a good way of life.

Most often, they explain their decision to live in a suburb rather than a city in terms of their family status. They believe that suburbs, if less attractive in location and cultural life, are still more desirable than cities for raising their children:

> A great thing about Hillcrest is its access—the commute is very good. My number one preference would be to live in San Francisco, but I feel with a family and three children I prefer not to live in the city, with the school systems and the things that go on. I just don't think that a city's a very good environment for children. This is a very good community to raise children in. The schools are excellent—the family atmosphere. So when my children grow up, I would like to move back to the city.
>
> In cities there's the hustle and bustle. And in San Francisco, obviously, the sophistication. The type of business people in San Francisco are quite knowledgeable. And I like it because of all the activities: I like to do things rather than staying home in the evenings and watching TV or playing cards. You can get out and go to an art museum or a nice restaurant. And there are more educational things in San Francisco so you're more knowledgeable as a human being.

And their attraction to the city may give their characterizations of suburbia an uneasy enthusiasm:

> Hillcrest is very suburban—kind of rural atmosphere, nice weather, overpriced, and the schools are very good. It lacks some things: there's not a whole lot for the young people to do.
>
> The people are—generally—well-educated, affluent, conservative, and suburban: they drive station wagons, play tennis, play bridge. All those things that are in the book of American Dreams. It's a very typical, upper-middle class, white community.
>
> American suburbs? It's a ranch house, two cars, kids who take all kinds of lessons: swimming lessons, tennis lessons. If you had to describe it to a foreigner, it would be hard. It's just normal—this is suburbia—the wives stay home and raise the kids, the husbands work, they play bridge, and have pools. . . .
>
> I don't know, it just seems that it's a rather narrow perspective. But it's typical and we've been told that this is what's attractive and everyone should strive for it. So here we are.

Competing Interpretations: Ideology and Suburbia

The suburban transformation of the American landscape following World War II engendered considerable debate among popular commentators and social scientists. Though partially concerned with the causes of rapid suburban growth, controversy primarily focused on the consequences of suburbanization for American life. While suburban promoters identified suburbia with the American Dream, critics of suburbia in the 1950s argued that suburbs—with their physical conformity and patterns of commuting—were creating a new and deleterious culture of conformity, privatism, conservatism, and alienation. In the 1960s social scientists entered the fray, proposing that suburbia was neither the cultural wasteland of the suburban critic nor the promised land of the suburban developer.

What is less apparent is that this public debate has been accompanied by a less visible daily commentary by contemporary Americans. In all likelihood, the larger public debate over suburbia—particularly the views of promoters and critics— has helped define the cultural imagery of suburban life and has influenced the discourse of Americans about suburbs. What is certain, however, is that both the public debate and the everyday discussions about suburban life involve a cultural transformation—an attempt to identify and interpret the meaning of the suburban phenomenon.

Community ideologies have clearly been at the center of this cultural process, influencing the popular interpretations of suburbia volunteered by residents of San Francisco, Hillcrest, Bayside, and Valleytown. Suburban, urban, and small-town ideology each portray the suburb, though to differing degrees and in remarkably different ways. Suburban ideology presents the suburb as a clean, quiet, natural, secure community, with domesticity as the integrating motive of suburban life. With its access to urban amenities, suburbia escapes the provincialism and oppressiveness of small-town life; with its smaller scale and natural environment, it avoids the tension, pollution, and danger of the city. Suburbia is, in the language of suburban ideology, *"the best of both worlds."*

As we have seen in the previous two chapters, suburbia does not hold such a privileged position in the landscapes of small-town and urban ideology. In the symbolic landscape of the town, the suburb has not yet become a significant locale. When Villagers in Valleytown are queried about suburbs, they usually have little to say. And when they venture a description, suburbs are portrayed as fundamentally similar to either cities or small towns—and hence either undesirable or moderately agreeable places.

Suburbs are an important element in the ideology of the city, although their place in the metropolitan landscape receives two quite different interpretations. On the one hand, Urbanists may accentuate the fact that suburbs, through their proximity to cities, participate in urban life and culture. Suburbs are then placed in a middle ground between the excitement, opportunity, liberality, and freedom of the city—and the provincialism, oppressiveness, and traditionalism of the town. On the other hand, other Urbanists place the suburb in a no-man's-land between the amenities of urban life and the limited virtues of the town. Here, the conflict of city and suburb is expressed culturally, with Urbanists as the popular critics of suburbia. With cities portrayed as places of excitement, diversity, opportunity, tolerance, and individual freedom, suburbs become the locus of boredom, uniformity, conformity, conservatism, and moral estrangement.

The elaboration of such different images of suburban life in popular ideologies of place has meant, in turn, that individuals in different social and cultural contexts can and do articulate widely different views of suburbia. As one such context, community, itself, does make a difference: the idyllic image of suburbia is most often expressed by residents of Hillcrest and Bayside; the caustic view of the suburban critic, by residents of San Francisco. However, I have also proposed that suburban ideology is not so pervasive in suburbs as to define the meaning of suburbia for many suburban residents. In Bayside, some working-class residents with rural backgrounds are Suburban Villagers who think of themselves as small-town residents and who are oblivious to the suburban context. Other Suburban Villagers identify suburbia with suburban housing tracts and exclude their own suburban community from the suburban context. Still other residents of Hillcrest and Bayside—usually former city dwellers, often marginal in age or family status— think of their community as a suburb, but they describe it through an ambivalent or critical imagery of urban ideology. In short, though suburban ideology has become part of the cultural repertoire of community ideologies, it has apparently not yet become a significant ideological context for interpreting community life for substantial numbers of suburbanites. As a result, suburban residents living in the same place may conceptualize their community as a suburb or a small town and, in doing so, may describe its virtues—or vices—in remarkably different ways.

Part III

The Uses of Community Ideology

Chapter 6

Community Apologetics: Ideology, Accounts, and Community Problems

> She told him about her childhood on a farm and of her love for animals, about country sounds and country smells, and of how fresh and clean everything in the country is. She said that he ought to live there and that if he did, he would find that all his troubles were city troubles.
>
> Nathaniel West,
> *Miss Lonelyhearts*, 1962.

> Several authors in this present volume... explicitly question the belief that urban life contributes to social alienation and disorganization. Unquestionably, however, a majority of the general population and policy-makers accepts the hypothesis as an established axiom.
>
> J. John Palen,
> *City Scenes*, 1981.

Ideology and Community Problems

To many Americans, cities are virtually synonymous with urban problems. According to a national survey (HUD, 1978), approximately nine out of ten citizens believe that cities, compared to suburban, small-town, and rural communities, have the most crime. Eight out of ten charge that cities are the worst place to raise children; two out of three, that cities have less friendly people, the worst housing, the worst schools, and the most divorce.

Villagers in Valleytown would find such opinion data
rather unremarkable. If anything, some might well be sur-
prised that this indictment of city life was not even more
broadly shared. As we saw in chapter 3, Villagers conceive of
cities through a symbolic perspective that opposes urban life
to the virtues of the town. In this landscape, cities are a locus
of community problems, while the town remains a haven,
where the simple, good life of community still thrives.

Urbanists, however, would certainly find such popular
views more troubling. As we saw in chapter 4, Urbanists do
not routinely describe cities in terms of urban problems—of
crowding, pollution, failing schools, crime, and moral impoverishment. Rather, Urbanists articulate a popular ideology of
urban life in which cities are the place where the good life is
possible: exciting; full of cultural, social, and economic opportunity; liberal; a place of individual fulfillment. When community problems are used to define the essential features of the
place landscape, suburban and small-town life take center
stage. To the Urbanist, suburbs are less a symbol of the American dream than of the American mass: lacking identity, excessively conservative, personally alienating. To the Urbanist,
small towns are less a symbol of American community than of
provincialism, traditionalism, and social constraint.

Such contrasting imagery suggests the power of community ideology to interpret—and in doing so, to rationalize—
community problems. By framing the qualities of community
life within a symbolic landscape of virtues and vices, community ideology determines the cultural tracks along which
popular discourse moves. This process, however, runs even
further than might be assumed. Community ideologies not
only provide adherents with a sharp, vivid sense of *what* communities are like; they also provide Urbanists, Villagers, and
Suburbanists with a sense of *why* they are the way they are.
Ideologies, in short, involve a popular theory of the "workings" of community, providing *accounts that can be used to
explain community problems.*

Community accounts are important for two reasons. First,
such accounts, when framed within the perspective of community ideology, are not "disinterested." Just as community
ideology portrays the landscape of small-town, urban, and
suburban life in a manner that furthers community interests,
community accounts explain community problems in a way

that further legitimates such interests. Accounts accomplish this symbolic work by depicting the claims of ideology as the necessary workings of community. For example, small-town ideology accounts for the virtues of the town—and the vices of the city—by linking them to other "natural" and "inherent" features of town and city life. Thus, to the Villager, small towns are superior to cities, not because of some accident of history, the capriciousness of human nature, or the battles of local or national politics, but because small towns, as a type of community, produce a superior way of life. Within the perspective of the town, small towns become not only the locus but also the *source of the good life.*

Second, in the same manner that community accounts provide *cognitive authority for social interests,* they also *legitimate emotional ties to community.* By drawing on the accounts of a community ideology, adherents are able to rationalize their feelings about different forms of community. Though ideology of any form is often criticized for its ability to promote strong—and to the nonadherent, apparently irrational—emotional commitment, the ideology's capacity to produce and sustain commitment arises precisely because the ideological perspective does, to the adherent, "make sense" of an otherwise unaccountable world. Community accounts, in short, reinforce and legitimate commitment to community precisely because they help *make sentiment sensible.*

How, then, do community residents use community ideology to assess and account for community problems? How do such accounts further legitimate community interest and sentiment? We will explore these questions by taking an in-depth look at the varied ways Villagers and Urbanists assess two traditional areas of community concern: the relative friendliness and safety of small-town and city life.

Accounting for Friendliness

Cities are unfriendly places—or so it is said. The popular media abound with contemporary images of urban impersonality: the city visitor in need of help is greeted with vacant stares and brusque replies; the busy urbanite hurries home through the crowded street; the elderly woman sits alone in a musty hotel room; the homeless man wanders the street without a friend. As noted above, contemporary public opinion research also indicates that many Americans believe that people in cities are less friendly than people in other places. One survey, which asked Americans whether city, suburb, town, or farm "offers the friendliest people," reported that 13 percent selected the city, while 49 percent chose a rural small town or a farm, 21 percent selected a suburb, and 16 percent indicated there was no difference between places or that they were not sure (HUD, 1978).[1]

Belief in the superior friendliness of town life, it should be noted, is not without some foundation in experience. On the one hand, scientific studies of the willingness of town and city people to help others indicate that small-town people are somewhat more likely to offer aid to strangers (Milgram, 1970). This urban reserve to the stranger appears attributable to the urbanite's fear of crime, the etiquette of urban public behavior, and cultural conflict between diverse urban social groups, but not to differences in the personality of small-town and city residents. On the other hand, studies of the personal networks of people in city and town indicate that people in small towns do not, on average, have more social ties than people in cities. Although small-town residents are more likely to be involved with kin than city folks, urbanites are no more isolated, having more ties to people at work, in secular associations, and to individuals met in other contexts (Fischer, 1982, 1984; Reiss, 1959).

Villagers: "Naturally, People Are Friendlier in Towns"

Few Villagers doubt that people are friendlier in small towns than in cities. Relative newcomers to Valleytown sometimes note that small-town people may be a bit "reserved" with outsiders moving into their community. This reserve, however, is seen as only temporary, and it is thought of as symptomatic of the strength—rather than weakness—of community in the small town:

> People moving to a small town shouldn't get discouraged with the people. It's hard to get in with them real fast in a small town. Almost everybody's related to everybody and they don't accept outsiders too well. But once they do accept you, they'll help you all the way. You just have to be patient with them and show them you're not going to hurt the community or anything.

The Villager's ready espousal of the friendliness of the town is not simply grounded in experience but in shared beliefs about the very workings of town and city life. They routinely propose that town and city life make it likely for people—whatever their disposition or personality—to act in a more friendly manner in small towns than in cities. Often, Villagers note that the town's small size and easygoing pace "make it natural" for people in the town to be friendly to each other:

> People are friendlier in small towns. I think it's the town, itself. In town things are slower. The people stay, they have roots. Mainly the slow pace, and naturally, they're friendlier since they know everybody from somewhere.

They may also suggest that cities, lacking these conditions, necessarily have unfriendly people:

> The city has too many people, too much going on, all mixed in too fast. City people are too busy doing other things to be friendly. Country people, they sit back and enjoy life.

One Villager, deliberating cautiously on the differences in behavior she sees, even speculates that city people might be more friendly if size did not make it impossible to "know everybody" in the city:

> It's hard to say how friendly people really are in a city, but probably less than a small town. When we go to the city, we stay with our daughter's family and we meet her friends. In a small town it's friendly because you run up against the same people all the time. In a city you wouldn't do that. Perhaps if you did, they would be just as friendly as in a town.

Villagers may also note that the small size of the town sustains other conditions that encourage people to be friendly. People are not only apt "to know everybody" in the town; they are also likely to share interests with other members of the town:

> People are friendlier in small towns because there're fewer people and they have more in common. They share the same interests, like in Valleytown, ranching.

... and to engage in common activities:

> People in cities are less friendly. If you're walking down the
> street, nobody says, "Hi!" That's probably because small-
> town people are seeing the same people more and are in-
> volved with them in the same activities—community
> activities, whatever. So they're going to have more of a
> chance to be exposed to one another and to be friendly.

Inherent differences in the size and pace of town and city
life may even be thought to produce differences in outlook and
personality of town and city people, differences that lead to
variation in friendliness. The "hectic" pace of city life may
make city people more nervous and, hence, less friendly than
small-town people:

> Cities are less friendly because of the way life is geared in a
> city as opposed to a small town. It's geared much higher.
> You're going at a much faster clip. You've got more tensions
> and pressures to deal with. More things to irritate you. Be-
> cause of that, people in cities tend to be a bit more on edge.

The size and anonymity of the city—where no one knows
anybody—is said to provide little motivation for mutual concern, which when habitual, may result in general indifference
to others:

> Cities are very unfriendly. Seems to me city people would
> rather turn around and not talk to you as to have to say, "Hi!"
> The bigger a place gets, the more you lose your identity. If
> you run into people you're never going to see again, you
> don't care about what kind of character you're portraying or
> how you come across. In a small town you're running into
> people so you just want to put forward a better foot. In a big
> town, why bother to make an effort?

This lack of common life and mutual concern produces
the "self-centered" orientation of the city person who
"doesn't have time for others" and is overconcerned with personal needs:

> I think people in small towns are a lot friendlier than cities—
> and a bit nosier, too [chuckles]. It's because the town is

smaller. When there's more people in a town, they've got more to do and they don't care about the other person as much. Smaller communities got more time to talk to their neighbors. Bigger communities have more to do, and the people are more self-centered with their own problems. They haven't got the time to be involved. Even in churches. If you go to a big one there, they're less concerned.

Finally, some Villagers suggest that the superior friendliness of town life is part of small-town culture passed on from generation to generation. The friendly, concerned outlook of small-town people is nurtured in the small-town person's childhood, as well as the current condition of the town:

> People are friendlier in a small town. If someone was in trouble, they would be more likely to get help than in a large city. . . . I think it's just part of growing up in a small town, of living here so many years. As you are growing up, you are taught to help someone, to be friendly, yourself.

Urbanists: "City People Are as Friendly as You Want Them To Be"

To Urbanists, the assertion that city people are less friendly than small-town people requires interpretation at two levels. If regarded as true, it needs to be "made sense of," like other community differences. Moreover, because the belief has pejorative implications for both city life and city residents, it calls for an account that—if possible—discounts the belief's unfavorable implications.

Urban ideology, unlike the ideology of the town, does not directly address the purported impersonality of city life. As a result, in describing city life and city people, Urbanists do not volunteer the view that city people are any more—or less—friendly than people in other places. If questioned on the matter, they respond in several ways. First, a few Urbanists comment that city people are, in fact, more friendly than people in other places. Like the following working-class Urbanist, they may argue that the opportunities of urban life help city people to develop interpersonal skills that exceed those of people in other places:

> People are friendlier in cities than in small towns. They're used to a lot of people. If they have the disposition to be friendly, they're going to be in a city. They're more outgoing,

more confident. It's the big city background. I'm friendly and
I meet people easily.

Second, other Urbanists propose that people in cities,
suburbs, and small towns are equally friendly, or that such
comparisons simply "do not make sense." In the latter case,
they stress that particular cities and towns vary much more
in friendliness than do types of places, even denying the existence of any significant differences in friendliness between
types of places:

> Some people say that city people are more aggressive and
> pushy. Maybe you have that on the East Coast, but I don't
> detect that in San Francisco or Los Angeles. Rural people
> can be just as nasty. . . . I think there are differences by ac-
> tual community, but not by cities and towns. Two places I
> lived, they were both suburbs, they had the same housing
> density, but they differed a lot.

More often, Urbanists reluctantly note that people are
probably more friendly in small towns than in cities, although
they may immediately add that small-town people are more
friendly to each other than to "outsiders" from other communities. These Urbanists explain this difference in terms of the
different conditions that city and small-town residents face in
their daily lives, never in terms of basic differences in personality between city and small-town people. Moreover, the particular aspects of urban and small-town life that Urbanists select
to account for this contrast in behavior are also likely to be
different from those of the Villager. Typically, Urbanists propose that the danger of crime in the city precludes an outgoing, friendly style of interaction among city residents:

> People are most friendly in a small town 'cause they have
> less to fear. There are a lot of people in this city who have
> had bad experiences—muggings, what have you. Therefore,
> they're going to be a little held back. It's a self-protective
> thing.

Urbanists may mention the pace of city life and urban
crowding, but such accounts are offered less frequently than
by Villagers. The dominant account that Urbanists use to explain the behavior of city people is fear of crime, not frustra-

tion or indifference. In addition to crime, Urbanists may note other conditions that make city people less likely to act friendly than small-town people. Some contend that the built environment of city life, particularly apartment house living, is less conducive to interacting with other people in a casual manner:

> Cities vary a good deal in how friendly they are. San Francisco is very friendly, but other large cities are less so. There are probably more people who live in apartments, which are not conducive to "leaning over the back fence" or meeting someone while you're mowing the lawn. Also, the problem of crime makes people fearful.

Most significantly, Urbanists may also contend that urban impersonality has a different meaning than first appears when analyzed in terms of its underlying causes. Commenting on the town, an Urbanist may suggest that small towns are friendly because of their provincialism and social constraints rather than the vitality of their community:

> People in small towns are more friendly because they've got nothing else to do [chuckles]. People knock on the door and bring flowers and casseroles—that sort of thing. There are parties, backyard get-togethers. There aren't that many other things to do.

Another Urbanist, drawing on the ideology of the city, argues that any differences are symptomatic of the respect for privacy and personal freedom that urban life encourages:

> Where people are friendly depends on what you mean. In small towns, people can be "very friendly" [chuckles] but to me it's unfriendly—it's an intrusion. Cities are friendly, and suburbs, obnoxious, neutral, no neither. Not even neutral, because I think they're phony.

Such arguments may take on substantial complexity. An Urbanist, for instance, may reject the belief that people are more friendly in towns than in cities; yet, at the same time, use the imagery of urban ideology to argue that the friendliness of city people is a product of the freedom of city life while that of small-town people is a symptom of social constraint:

> I think people are as friendly as you want them to be. It's a
> two-way street. If you're friendly, they'll be friendly. I think
> they're friendly in small towns because they have to be. If
> they're not, there's a stigma, they get a certain reputation. In
> suburbs, that means there's children involved. So you are
> forced to be more friendly than you want to be. You're in-
> volved as neighbor's parents, in Scouts, schools, etc. Factors
> force you. Small towns and suburbs force you, where in cities
> you have what you want to give.

Or urbanists may reject the "problem" of urban impersonality because they believe that city people are "both" more
and less friendly than small-town people. Admitting that the
impersonality of urban public life is a reality, they also claim
that the liberality of the city makes people "really" more open
than people elsewhere:

> The social habits are different in a city. In a small town, you'd
> probably smile at someone and say "Good morning" as you
> walk by. While in a city this is something you would not do,
> or if you did, you might be considered very strange and have
> a disagreeable experience. So as you walk down the street,
> you don't take it personally.
> I don't mean to say that people in a city would be less
> really friendly but that they would have different mores in
> "being friendly." On the surface, you might think that a
> small-town person is friendlier from his behavior. From my
> own experience, once you've got into the Zen of how people
> communicate in the city, they can be really friendly. Like in
> New York, people can be. But it has to be in the right kind of
> way—the socially acceptable way, and that's very different
> than in the country. . . . After that, city people may be even
> more friendly 'cause they're more open.

Accounting for Safety and Crime

The image of the city as a place of danger is a recurring
theme in the history of urban imagery. In their essay on antiurban ideology, Hadden and Barton (1973) propose that this
association is as old as the Judeo-Christian tradition in Western culture. In the Old Testament, the city represents a place
of escape from God's rule and judgment and, hence, a place of
profound spiritual peril. In American culture, cities have been
regarded as dangerous places since colonization, although

different risks have been associated with urban life at different periods in American history. Seventeenth-century Puritans feared the city as a threat to traditional social order and spiritual virtue (Rutman, 1965; Bushman, 1970). To Thomas Jefferson, cities—with their urban mobs—posed a political threat to civil society (Rourke, 1964). Late in the nineteenth century reformers believed the immigrant ghettos, industrial conflict, and social disorder of the industrial city endangered both the physical and moral well-being of the individual. Today, many Americans continue to think of cities as dangerous places, although the danger of urban life is now more likely associated with criminal violence than with a spiritual, political, or moral threat. As noted above, nine out of ten Americans in a national survey believe cities "offer the most crime" of any type of place (HUD, 1978).

Popular belief in the superiority of town over city in crime and safety is grounded in contemporary reality as well as the cultural legacy. Although cities are probably safer today than they were a hundred years ago (Lane, 1968), contemporary urban crime rates are high, and for most types of crime, they exceed those of suburb, town, and country. While higher crime rates in cities may be due in part to better administration of crime statistics in cities, urban-rural differences are certainly real. Survey studies, for instance, indicate that city residents are more likely to report being a victim of a crime, and they are more likely to fear for their safety in public than are residents of other places.[2]

Villagers: "Things Are Bound to Happen in Cities"

To Villagers, whose conceptions of the community landscape are largely defined by the ideology of the town, personal safety is a salient difference between city and town. Small towns are nearly always thought to be safer than cities, and to some Villagers cities may be regarded as so perilous as to be virtually uninhabitable:

> To tell the truth, I'd be scared to death to live in a city! It's very unsafe. I mean, we take the San Francisco *Examiner* and watching TV news—it seems real dangerous.

Villagers easily marshal a variety of accounts to explain the relative safety of the town, most of which interpret the su-

periority of the town in terms of favorable qualities of town life
or the known deficiencies of city life. First, Villagers often attribute the safety of the town to community size. The greater
number of people in cities is thought to increase either the
volume or the rate of crime, but both outcomes are thought to
make cities less safe. Villagers believe size of community so
decisive that they may use size differentials to explain changing conditions within the town as well as to account for differences between city and town:

> Cities are more dangerous than towns because of numbers—
> numberwise. And more crowded conditions, more people in a
> smaller area. Because I think your crime increases with the
> number of people. I think that is one of the reasons Valley-
> town is not as safe as it used to be. It has grown.

Second, Villagers believe cities are less safe because they
are "overcrowded" as well as "overpopulated." Urban population densities, typically thought of as crowded, are believed to
generate crime directly:

> From reading the paper, I'd say cities are unsafe to very un-
> safe to live in. The condensity [sic] of the people there, you've
> got more people together there. They've got less places to
> go to get away from each other; more things are bound to
> happen.

Few Villagers offer further explanation of how crowding
produces violent behavior, and when queried, they may simply
note that "it's just a feeling I have." One college-educated
Villager, however, added "scientific" evidence to back up his
belief:

> Cities are less safe because of what people have to cope with
> in everyday life—it makes for conditions where you tend to
> see increased crime, violence. I recall where they've done
> studies with rat populations. When they really get overpopu-
> lated and crammed-up, they fight. It's cramping their life-
> style, and in situations like that you'll see aggression
> increase. . . . You can draw a parallel between the two. What
> they have to cope with.

Third, Villagers also attribute the crime of cities to the
"social and cultural disorganization" of city life. The urban

environment—with its hectic pace, its impersonality, and its frustration—is thought to increase crime:

> I think I saw more violence in the city than any other place I've worked. The environment that people have to live in in a large metropolis tends to make for an added increase in violence. Just the pressure of coping: like the traffic, and the people being impersonal with one another and not really giving a darn. That's basically it.

Cities, with their cultural permissiveness, lack the moral integrity of the town:

> Crime's more tolerated in the city. If you steal a purse in Valleytown, you can just about guess that you'll be turned in, while if you do it in San Francisco, they wouldn't even bother to turn you in. It's just one of those things. It's accepted. The people who are committing crimes are not tolerated by people as much in a small community as they are in a larger community.

Such urban disorganization and its attendant crime may even be seen as incomprehensible; yet this only serves to underline the basic disorder and irrationality of city life:

> People fight a lot more in cities, for no reason. Around here they sit down and talk about it; there, for no reason. Around here, cowboys do fight some, but they fight over things like cows and horses, which is their property. My grandfather, he owned land, and he fought for it, and you can relate to that. But in cities, they fight over nothing, over politics, things that they don't know nothing about. Seems like they've got nothing to do but pick on each other, or on kids. I've seen a lot of abuse on kids in cities. In the countryside, if you get hassled, you just keep them outside.

Such malaise, once established in the city, perpetuates itself:

> There's more crime in cities because there's more people and more to pick from in a city. I know if you've lived in a big city all your life, there's just more of an opportunity to get into things—to get into trouble—than there is in a small town.

Finally, Villagers explain the crime of cities in terms of other social and economic factors that are not necessarily considered intrinsic to city life. For instance, they sometimes propose that the "type of people" who live in cities—particularly, the poor, unemployed, and minorities—also contributes to making cities unsafe places:

> Cities have more crime because of the crowded conditions and because of the different elements of people who live there. Cities have their slum areas. People come looking for work, and they can't find it, so you have situations like that. A small town doesn't have people coming there thinking they're going to find a job.

Such explanations do not necessarily remove the onus of urban crime from the city, because the attractiveness of the city to criminals is, in turn, seen as a symptom of the problems of urban life. Cities may be said to draw the wrong type of people:

> Cities are like a magnet. A lot of people who commit crimes, they don't like a small town. Because the things they like or are looking for are in big cities. Especially the younger people—they are doing a lot of the crimes.

Cities may be characterized as places of transience and crime:

> Cities have more crime because they attract more transients, too. They go to see what a big city is like, and they hang around for awhile. You don't get such people coming to a small town to hang around. To them, it's a little nothing place.

Thus cities at once create conditions conducive to crime and, at the same time, attract people who are likely to get into trouble:

> Quite a few things make cities have more crime. I suppose that part of it is that some of the people who couldn't make it in the small towns gravitate to the city, and they're violent prone. And there's that live in the city all their life and never

aspire to anything above that. And there's lack of parental control, though kids from the same family can go different ways.

Nearly all Villagers thus believe that cities are much more dangerous places to live than small towns and that urban crime can be explained in part by the inherent size, density, and disorder of city life and in part by the kinds of people who are attracted to cities. Two Villagers, however, commented that small towns are also dangerous places. Although unusual, these Villagers are the exceptions that prove the rule: their accounts, again, only reiterate the importance of small-town ideology. One such Villager, alarmed by crime in Valleytown, attributes the source of crime to city life. Small towns, she argues, are becoming less safe because urban criminals are becoming more mobile:

> I don't think it's any safer to live in a small town than a big city, because we get hoodlums here from all over. In fact, there was a man here who peeked in our windows. And it turned out that he didn't live here—he lives in some city— he's just down here visiting. You got to lock your windows now wherever you live.

The other Villager, who had been personally confronted with the reality of a serious crime in Valleytown, no longer finds the traditional accounts of small-town ideology compelling. Lacking an alternative interpretation, she suggests that life seems less rational—and accountable—than it used to:

> Small towns are safer than cities, but not safe. We had a murder here, which was quite a shocker for all of us who thought that small towns were safe. And here again, it was someone that most people knew, not like a city where you'd read about someone on a streetcar or something. *Everything is quite unpredictable it seems.*

Urbanists: "Cities Are Safe, But it Depends"

To Villagers, the danger of living in cities is both an essential quality of city life and a symptom of the deeper, inherent problems of urban life. Urbanists, however, when describing the community landscape, do not point to crime as an essen-

tial characteristic of city life. Whatever the immediate reality
of urban crime, such beliefs are not part of the perspective of
urban ideology, and do not come as readily "to mind" to Urbanists as they do to Villagers living in a small-town or suburban community.

How, though, do Urbanists analyze this matter that others
believe so characteristic of American city life? If directly queried about crime and community life, a few Urbanists actually
propose that cities are safer than other places. Such Urbanists do not deny that urban residents face problems with
crime, but they also maintain that suburban and small-town
residents encounter comparable or greater problems. According to the following working-class Urbanist, for example, the
organizational capacity and diversity of cities enables cities to
deal with problems of crime more effectively than other
places:

> I think small towns and suburbs may be harder hit by prob-
> lems than cities. They have more problems. Like controlling
> crime. Their police manpower is smaller. They don't have the
> investigative teams like they do here in the city. And they
> don't have that many different types of people. If they have a
> lot of criminals, they don't have enough good people to com-
> bat it. A big city has a balance, more or less. It can control
> itself. In this district, for instance, we can get together and
> keep the elements from getting out of hand, like with block
> organizations.

The assertion that cities are as safe or even safer than
other places may be substantiated by a description of the
risks posed by living other places. To the following Urbanist,
who partially rejects comparisons between places for crime,
suburbs are clearly also perilous places to live:

> The suburbs, like Orange County in Los Angeles, they're get-
> ting a very high crime rate now. It's all single-family homes,
> but it can be a very unsafe place to be. You just can't say
> cities or suburbs are safer; you also have to know the type of
> crime. When I was in college, I wrote a theme on the decay of
> suburbia. In suburbia, you're just as likely to be ripped off,
> burglary is rampant. There's nobody on the street by defini-
> tion, and if anything is going to happen, nobody's going to
> see it. There's a real epidemic of rape. The safety is illusory.

> Criminals are learning about suburbia and they go wild: bur-
> glaries, the houses are easy to break into, there's nobody
> home or on the street, the neighbors are too far away, and
> there's a lot of wealth. It's a great place for ripping off.

This belief in the relative dangers of other places led one
Urbanist to remark that he feels safest in the midst of the pop-
ulous city:

> Suburbs are just as hazardous as cities in terms of burglar-
> ies and property. I think small towns may be even a little
> more dangerous from what people were telling me of robber-
> ies. Personally, I really feel more safe in an apartment build-
> ing, here, than I do in somebody's house out in the middle of
> nowhere. If something happens, I know there are people
> nearby. Out in the country, there's nobody around. That's
> where I feel unsafe. Even more in the wilderness than in a
> small town where at least you'd have a neighbor.

More often, Urbanists reject comparisons of cities with
other places for matters of crime and safety. Unlike Villagers,
they may directly contend that cities, suburbs, and small
towns do not vary significantly in their relative safety. Because Urbanists usually regard cities as safe places, they may
suggest that cities and towns—*however different they are in
other respects*—are similar in the basic security they offer
their residents:

> Cities, suburbs, and small towns are all safe. I don't think
> that society could survive if things were really unsafe. The
> news gives you the impression that cities are unsafe, but
> people couldn't tolerate it, if it were really unsafe: if you
> didn't know whether you were coming back alive. I don't
> know anybody who's been mugged. I know it happens, and it
> can happen to me, but you expect to have your physical
> safety and peace of mind.

Urbanists who believe that types of places do not vary significantly in their safety may argue that such comparisons
simply do not "make sense." They may, for example, propose
that particular cities vary from one to another so greatly that
generalizations about the danger of cities are meaningless:

> You have to qualify what city you're talking about when you
> talk about how safe cities are. San Francisco is generally
> safe. In Detroit, once when I was Christmas shopping, a
> young fellow came racing through the store brandishing a
> stupendous knife. I can't even conceive of that in downtown
> San Francisco. If you lived in Portland, it might be some-
> where between two extremes—between San Francisco and
> Detroit. It's tough to say 'cause all cities are different.

Or they may propose that neighborhoods within cities
vary so greatly in their safety that characterizations of the
danger of cities are wrongheaded:

> To say how safe a city is you have to know the neighborhood.
> San Francisco is like that. There are a few bad areas in a
> city—usually around the Greyhound Bus Station [laughs].
> But then there's Pacific Heights, which is a low crime area,
> and it's right next to Fillmore, which has a lot of crime.
> There's the kind of crime, too. In the Mission, that's a poor
> area so there's burglary and a lot of bar fights. So don't go to
> the bars: that'll solve a lot of your problems.

To the extent that the locus of crime is interpreted primarily in terms of neighborhood rather than the city, an Urbanist
may even construe some of the risks of city life as simply a
matter of fate:

> Cities, suburbs, towns—they're all safe. There are districts in
> cities that aren't, but if you're stupid enough to trot around
> in them, you're asking for trouble. If crime happens to get
> into your district, you're out of luck. You're one of the unfor-
> tunate ones who got caught at the wrong place at the wrong
> time. The Zodiac, he shot a girl two blocks from here.

Finally, some Urbanists note that cities have more crime
than suburbs and small towns and, as a result, are relatively
less safe places to live. They may account for the greater danger of cities in terms of the greater population of cities,
though they suggest this account less frequently than do Villagers. Such size, they indicate, creates anonymity conducive
to crime:

> Cities are not that safe anymore. Small towns are safer be-
> cause you know a lot of people. You have a sense of what's
> going on. There's not a stranger walking on the street every

ten minutes. . . . There's so much going on in a city that your neighbor across the street doesn't necessarily know who's going in and out of your house. In a small town, they'd be reported if they saw a stranger going into your house.

The Urbanists with whom I spoke did not, however, typically account for such problems in terms of "overcrowding and overpopulation," the "hectic pace of city life," a "lack of concern" on the part of urbanites, or the moral impoverishment of urban culture. They may even volunteer direct challenges to such popular accounts of urban crime:

> People always say the density of the area has something to do with there being more crime in cities, but that isn't true. If you look at Europe, Germany is one of the most densely populated countries in the world, but the crime rate is much lower than it is here. It may just be that the United States has reached its peak and is declining—like the Roman Empire.

And they may propose that such matters should be seen in a broader context than community. They note that urban crime must not be interpreted in terms of city life but the economic conditions faced by some city residents. In this account, crime is no longer a product of the city but of class inequality:

> Cities are less safe, though it's a relative risk factor. There may be as much property violence in suburbs, but I don't think there's as much physical violence as in cities. It has to do with the economic base of cities and suburbs. When you have that many deprived people in a small space who feel like they're being fucked over, you have a real problem. The roots of the revolution are in street crime, not politics.

They may even recast the apparent virtue of small-town safety into a possible vice, suggesting that the safety of the town is a product of the oppressiveness of small-town life, an oppressiveness that limits the just as well as the unjust:

> Small towns are much safer because they have a stable enough tax base to afford a few cops, and the cops in small towns can usually be grouped into the concept of "Deputy Dog": the kind that wears shiny sunglasses [chuckles]. What

I'm driving at is that the cops bear a lot of weight in the town, as opposed to a suburb or city where there's not this constant pervasive influence of the police. It's not as evident, and more things can be gotten away with. Tabs are much tighter in a small town.

Ideology, Explanation, and Commitment

If you directly ask Villagers and Urbanists about contemporary community problems, both have much to say. In the case of urban impersonality and crime, Villagers' answers come more easily than Urbanists, for the rhetoric of small-town ideology contains an extensive, appropriate litany of accounts for such problems. Nevertheless, both Villagers and Urbanists frame their interpretations of such problems within the perspective of opposing community ideologies, and in doing so, offer remarkably different assessments.

Villagers and Urbanists, we have seen, may simply disagree about the occurrence of a community problem. Although most Villagers are certain that people are both safer and friendlier in towns than in cities, some Urbanists suggest the opposite, contending that city people are more open to others than small-town people and that cities have better law enforcement capabilities. More often, Urbanists contend that cities and small towns—however different in other respects—do not vary significantly in terms of these community problems and that these comparisons, therefore, do not "make sense." For example, Urbanists may propose that particular cities or neighborhoods within cities vary so greatly in their safety and friendliness that generalizations about urban life are "not meaningful."

When Villagers and Urbanists concur about the existence of a community problem, they may still evaluate the degree of the problem quite differently and, most remarkably, differ in their explanation for the problem. Although some Urbanists believe cities to be less friendly and safe than towns, they do not, like some Villagers, propose that city people are overtly rude or that cities are so dangerous as to be virtually uninhabitable. Though some Urbanists recognize problems of crime and impersonality in the city, they attribute such problems to a different range of accounts than Villagers, accounts drawn from differing ideological perspectives.

This latter aspect of the interpretive process is most apparent in the different ways that Villagers and Urbanists conceptualize their accounts of the friendliness of people in town and city. Villagers, who identify the town with community, believe the size and pace of the town supports greater sociability and concern through the creation of common activities and interests. Villagers may even contend that the town—because of its culture and common life—produces a small-town personality that values others as well as self. Conversely, Villagers believe that cities lack such necessary conditions for the maintenance of community and, as a result, city people are simply indifferent to each other at best or callous at worst.

In contrast to Villagers, Urbanists may explain the greater sociability of the town through images of the city as a place of personal freedom and opportunity, and of the town as a community of constraint. Here, town folk are friendlier to each other because of social pressure, and small-town sociability becomes symptomatic of pettiness, gossip, and meddling rather than mutual concern. Townspeople are friendly to each other because they have "nothing else to do," constrained by the recreational opportunities of small-town life.

Though less dramatic and clear, Villagers and Urbanists use different patterns of accounts to explain the danger of cities. On the one hand, Villagers not only believe that cities are more dangerous than small towns; they also believe that the violence of cities is produced by the size, density, and intrinsic disorganization of urban life. Even when Villagers suggest that cities have more crime because they have come—through mobility—to have more minorities and poor people, they may simply imply that the attraction of cities to such people is also symptomatic of the inherent disorganization of city life. On the other hand, Urbanists are somewhat less likely to conceive of the crime of cities as inherent to urban life. Though they sometimes suggest that urban scale exacerbates crime through anonymity, they may challenge claims that city crime is a product of urban density or urban disorganization, offering alternative accounts that stress economic or other noncommunal sources of crime.

When viewed as a whole, the contrasting interpretations of community problems offered by Villagers and Urbanists underline the power of community ideology to further community interests and sentiment. Drawing on their ideological perspective, community apologists differ in their assessment of the existence and gravity of community problems and in the explanations they offer for those problems. Though no single account is necessarily remarkable in itself, these differences—when seen as shared systems of interpretation—are at once strategic and meaningful. More often than not, these interpretations of community problems only deepen the adherent's commitment to a community form, providing accounts that render their community the source of the good life. In doing so, community ideology legitimates personal sentiment and social interest through the apparent voice of reason.

Chapter 7

Community Identity[1]

> My point is that space robs identity. Place, on
> the other hand, nurtures it, tells you who you
> are—either "I belong" or "This is foreign to me,
> and I am an outsider."
>
> Orrin Klapp,
> *Collective Search for Identity*, 1969.

Beyond Placelessness

Former analyses of the fate of identity in modern urban
society have, for the most part, been pessimistic. This indictment has been most severe with respect to identities of place.
The modern individual—highly mobile, socially rootless, living in a gray landscape of sterile houses, mass-produced
neighborhoods, Manhattanized cities, and disappearing regions—has supposedly become homeless, with little sense of
the place in which he or she resides, little attachment to
home, neighborhood, settlement or region (Klapp, 1969; Packard, 1972; Relph, 1976; Stein, 1960; Webber, 1970; Wheelis,
1958; Wirth, 1938).

Recent research on various forms of place identity has
done much to undermine this indictment (Hummon, 1986c).
The home—along with its interior objects and exterior deco-
ration—often serves as a significant locus of self and a sign of
biographical, social, and temporal identities (Hummon, 1989;
Duncan, 1982; Csikzentimihali and Rochberg-Halton, 1981;
Perin, 1977; Cooper, 1974). Urban neighborhoods play a significant part in social order, public behavior, and identity in the

city (Hunter, 1974; Karp, Stone, and Yoels, 1977; Lofland, 1973; Rivlin, 1982; Suttles, 1968). Even regions may enrich place identity: those who identify with the South express both emotional attachment to their region and favorable imageries of southerners as friendly, traditional, gracious, good people (Reed, 1983). Newcomers to Alaska reinterpret their identity through interaction with long-term residents and local experiences and, in doing so, acquire a new sense of place and self (Cuba, 1987).

Despite this recent work, no research has directly explored the extent to which contemporary Americans use community ideology to construct a community identity: a sense of being a city person, suburbanite, small-town person, or country person. In this chapter, I will first explore this possibility, demonstrating that some contemporary Americans do appropriate the imagery of community ideology to define a rich and complex sense of self. Then, by comparing these individuals with those who lack such a clear sense community identification, I will further explore the complex ways that community ideology, mobility, and experience combine to produce widely different senses of community among contemporary Americans.

Identity and Ideology

Matters of identity involve a person's sense of self: self-reflexive answers to that ongoing, inescapable, and quintessentially human question, "Who am I?" As such, it involves a "positioning" of self in reality, a symbolic placement that situates the person in the world, at once differentiating the individual from some aspects of reality, affiliating the person with other aspects (Berger and Luckmann, 1967). Identity also involves an interpretation of the qualities of self, characterized in self-imagery. This dual nature of identity is reflected in the everyday language of identity and identification. We identify ourselves *as* people of a certain type, quality, or value; we also identify ourselves *with* others or with significant objects, forging a sense of belonging and attachment.

A *community identity* may be thus defined as *an interpretation of self that uses community as a locus of attachment or an image for self-characterization.* Like other forms of identity, community identity answers the question, "Who am I?" but does so by countering, "Where am I?" or, more fundamentally, "Where in the landscape of community forms do I belong?" It identifies the individual with place through the construction of ties to a form of community; it identifies the individual as a type of person by appropriating community imagery for self-imagery. Identification with the small town, for instance, involves both a sense of being "in place" in the town and a favorable conception of self as particularly "friendly," "neighborly," and "family-oriented," self-conceptions drawn from the imagery of small-town ideology.

Community ideology plays a critical role in this process. The symbolic landscape of community ideology provides a *convincing rendering* of *varied social, moral, and other qualities* of communities and their inhabitants, diverse qualities that can be appropriated for self-characterization. Its *favorable rendering* of these features, moreover, insures that appropriated images will *enhance self-esteem*, enabling the person to affirm the self and rationalize its relation to community. Finally, the ideology's systematic portrayal of a whole *landscape of places* provides the necessary framework for *symbolic placement of the self*, providing the symbolic structure for *affiliation and disaffiliation*.[2]

Identification with Community: On Being a City Person

When queried about community identity, some contemporary Americans readily respond, "I'm a city person." These individuals, whom I will call *City Folk*, are most likely to be current residents of cities, but not all residents of cities claim this identity. In San Francisco, approximately two out of three people designated themselves as a city person, with the remainder replying that they never thought of themselves in terms of any community identity (Table 3). Former city residents living elsewhere may also continue to identify with the city. In suburban Hillcrest and Bayside, this was the case with approximately one in four respondents.

City Folk often interpret their urban identity by describing their *sentimental ties* to cities. Some simply suggest that they enjoy cities more than other places:

> I'm a city person. I like living in the city. I like the hustle and
> bustle of the city, I guess. I like the different things to do. I
> sure don't think I'm too sophisticated for the country
> [laughs].

Other City Folk express stronger feelings of attachment to
cities, noting their sense of being "in place" or "out of place"
through contrasts with other forms of community. Like individuals describing the experience of being "at home" in a locality (Seamon, 1979), these individuals describe cities as
places where one feels particularly "at ease" or "comfortable":

> I'm a city person. Even when I lived in a suburb of Buffalo, I
> was a city person. I just didn't fit. I'm comfortable in a city. I
> like the close proximity, the potential excitement of what's
> going on.

They may also express doubts about their ability to "fit into"
other places:

> I think of myself as a city person, very definitely. I have lived
> in San Francisco all this time and like it. You adapt to the
> ways of the city. I don't have too much time. I'm working, and
> I go about my own business. In a small town, you'd get to
> know people, and it's quiet and slower paced. I don't know
> whether I could adjust to that.

For a few City Folk, these sentimental ties constitute strong
and salient bonds of identification:

> I'm a city boy. I drive to work twenty-five miles each way—to
> the suburbs. . . . I live in the city because it has everything I
> need and want. I don't know whether I could live in the sub-
> urbs—"out on the lone prairie." I don't know because I love,
> need the pulse, the beat of the city, and the activity and the
> going down[town] shopping. I'm not a small-town boy where
> you have to walk around and say, "Howdy, Jack, and Smith,
> and Jane." I don't need that, though I have it.

City Folk also contend that they are a city person because
they have *interests* that they believe are particularly *appropriate to an urban way of life*. They want to be "where the action
is" or where there are "a lot of things to do." Others are more

Table 3: Community Identity by Community of Residence

Community of Residence

Community Identity	San Francisco	Bayside or Hillcrest	Valleytown	
city person	65%	23%	4%	
suburbanite	0	19	0	
small-town person	0	8	28	
country person	0	8	40	
no identity	35	42	28	
Total	100% (26)	100% (26)	100% (25)	(77)

Text of question: Do you think of yourself as a city person, a small-town person, a suburbanite, or a country person, or don't you think of yourself in such terms?

specific, noting either special interests in sophisticated cultural activities like the opera or a penchant for frequent use of stores, theaters, and restaurants. Such ties often provide the continuing basis of identification with the city for City Folk living in suburbs:

> I still think of myself as a city person. I like being in an area that has a lot of people and activity around me. I like to be able to walk out the door and jump on a bus and get to people without driving forty miles. I like being in an area that has a lot of restaurants, theaters, and cultural activities. That's what I grew up with, and that's what I enjoy. I can still go to the city, but out here you forget about it.
> [Do you ever think of yourself as a suburbanite?]
> No, I'm a city person, but I just happen to live in a suburb.

In addition to ties of sentiment and urban interests, some City Folk base their identity as a city person on a sense of *shared values* with other city people. Such values are routinely presented and explained as a product of the common experiences of urban residents, particularly those of growing up in the city. It may draw on urban ideology's identification of the city with creativity and open-mindedness:

> I'd been very different if I hadn't grown up in a city because the people I'd grown up with would have been so different. If I'd grown up in suburbia, I wouldn't have made my own entertainment, and I wouldn't have developed my own imagination. I wouldn't have seen my father so much, because he commutes. And I wouldn't have been aware. I would have grown up with stereotypes. In the city you grow up with all different types of people. In a small town, I'd still probably be there, and I'd probably be prejudiced.

Or it may appropriate urban ideology's portrayal of the city as a place of liberality and politics to interpret the self:

> My outlook on society is directly reflected in my childhood in San Francisco. I'm very liberal and that's just because I grew up here in San Francisco, period.
> I see myself as a city person in a kind of prejudicial way. I'm well-informed, knowledgeable about most things in general, aware of the situation politically. About everything I'm aware of, I think more aware of than a poor guy, the same age, from a place like Sacramento.

Finally, some City Folk base their identification with cities on their *knowledge of cities and urban life.* On the one hand, some City Folk, having spent most of their lives in cities, note that their knowledge of community life is largely limited to urban places. Like some long-term residents of a particular community who strongly identify with a particular locale because their sense of self is biographically embedded in a landscape of this place (Rowles, 1983a), these individuals, in a much more nominal way, experience themselves as in—and part of—the city. They "belong" in cities because cities are what they know—and only what they know. On the other hand, other City Folk base their identity directly on their knowledge of the norms of city life and their skills of dealing with urban situations—in short, their sense of an urban role and culture. Like Lofland's "urbane hero" (1973), they are skilled city residents who have mastered the techniques of urban interaction:

I'm a city person. I've had exposure to city life, I feel comfortable in the city, I can get around. I know how to deal with people on a very informal basis. There are certain rules: how to get along in a city, what to expect from people that you don't know. In a small town, I think there is much more of a personal level of what's expected. While in a city, you don't have that opportunity to get to know people that well. I think a lot of small-town people—that really throws them for a loop. They can't understand how everybody's just getting along.

Another individual, who has moved with his family to the suburbs, similarly bases his urban identity on his ability to deal with diverse groups of people in public settings:

I think of myself as potentially a country person, but I am a city person because I've lived there so much, and I've worked there so much. I have more city-sense: I can survive in the city easier than in the country.
　　[Do you think you have anything in common with city people?]
　　Oh, yes, knowing about the kind of people who live in the city and knowing how to cope with them. You have to be able to, especially if you drive a cab in the city like I do. If you can't stand homosexuals, you don't drive a cab in the city. I can cope with gay people, old people; I can cope with drunks.

The community identity of these City Folk suggests two general conclusions. First, "being a city person" provides some Americans with a sense of "belonging" because community identification involves the articulation of *ties to place.* Though this self-designation may have only nominal meaning for some who claim it, reflecting only residential status, for others it involves a subjective identification with cities, urban life, and people. Self-proclaimed city people anchor themselves in the urban context: they feel they "belong there." Such affiliation is most common among urban residents, but former city residents, living in suburb or town, may maintain their sense of urban identity.

Second, because identification with cities may involve one or more ties to place, community identity *varies considerably in strength and complexity.* Typically, identification involves *sentimental attachment* to cities, but it may also include an articulation of *urban interests*, a sense of *shared values* with other urban residents, and a *knowledge of urban life and role*. As a result, both the particular configuration of ties and the resulting strength of identification varies from person to person, with community identity ranging from an attenuated sense of emotional attachment to a relatively rich and complex investment of self in cities and urban life.

Community Identity as Self-Conception

If community identity involves a sense of belonging, it also incorporates a conception—and self-conception—of a type of person. Though no two City Folk describe their qualities as a city person in exactly the same way, collectively they present a "self-portrait" of people who are active, up-to-date, "culturally" oriented, imaginative, unprejudiced, aware, and citywise. This self-characterization clearly is framed within the shared perspective of urban ideology, a perspective that depicts the city as a place of culture, entertainment, civility, and liberalism. This translation of community imagery into self-imagery can be further illustrated by examining how people who identify with small-town, country, and suburban life use community ideology to formulate a favorable identity.

Town Folk

Images of small-town life and people are rich and variegated. In Valleytown, Villagers use small-town ideology to describe the town as a locus of community and a bastion of tradition, and in doing so, they propose that small-town people are particularly easygoing, friendly, neighborly, and concerned about family life. Within the metropolitan context, the image of town people is considerably less uniform and often less favorable. Urban critics of town life, drawing on urban ideology, frequently maintain that town people are excessively concerned with sociability, describing them as gossipy and petty rather than neighborly and concerned. Similarly, metropolitan residents treat the imagery of small-town tradition with greater ambivalence. They characterize—with considerable ambiguity—town people as more "conservative," not only in their emphasis on family life but also in their religious, political, and social outlook. For urban critics, such imagery leads to portrayals of town people as "backward," "narrow-minded," and "intolerant."

In Valleytown and suburban Hillcrest, some individuals, referred to below as *Town Folk*, identify with small-town life and people. Like City Folk, Town Folk feel they belong in a particular form of community, and they express ties of sentiment, interest, and value in characterizing their identity. Their self-image as a type of person, however, is appropriated from the positive imagery of small-town ideology as a place of community, domesticity, and tradition. Town Folk may define their identity in terms of the embeddedness of family life in communal relations:

> I'm a small-town person because I like living in a small town. Small-town people don't want all the hustle and bustle. They want to know people, to have close relations with a lot of families. People who are in small towns want their children in small schools. They want to know the families of the friends of their children. And the teachers—they might be your neighbor, or you bump into them at gatherings.

This imagery of family life, community, and its attendant sociability is also routinely used to account for the open, outgoing, friendly qualities of self and other:

> Valleydale, where I grew up, was a small community. I think a small community is more ideal because it's probably a bit more closer knit. Things are done in groups—and with friends.
>
> [Do you think growing up in a small community has influenced you?]
>
> Oh, I think it has to influence you some. Coming from that situation I knew just about everyone. In a bigger city you wouldn't have that—it's more distant. So growing up there was a good experience and that has an effect: it might make you more people-oriented.

Or, when questioned about how they might have been different had they grown up in a city, several Town Folk imagined that they might well have been less sociable and concerned about others:

If I'd grown up in a city? I think I'd be different though I can't speak from experience. I would probably be less sensitive, less personable, less wanting to get involved with things in general. That's an impression I have.

Although these central images draw upon the portrayal of the town as place of community and sociability, Town Folk also use their negative conceptions of the city, drawn from small-town ideology, to clarify their identity. They may assert that their identification is based on a rejection of the interests and values of city people. Typically, they note that a small-town person—with interests in family and friends—"doesn't need" the excitement, entertainment, and activity that a "city person does":

I'm more of a small-town person. I'm more of a home person. I enjoy my home life and my friends; I don't need to be entertained. A city person has to be entertained. Family, friends, home.

Such contrasts may also imply that "being a small-town person" entails a rejection of such spurious "urban" values as materialism or conformity:

I'm a small-town person. You're not into materialistic things so much. You're not worried about how you're dressed or whether you have the latest clothes on. That's one thing I noticed when I go to San Francisco. Everybody's got on capes and boots and things like that. We're more for comfort.

Lack of such negative qualities, like more favorable aspects of identity, can also be attributed to childhood in a small town:

Growing up in a small town was perfect: the country atmosphere, the small town, knowing everybody, and my parents, they had a business. If I'd grown up in a larger city, I'd been more materialistic. 'Cause you have to have more things. You're happier in a small town, closer to the earth: you grew your own vegetables. We'd play outside. We had acres to play on, so I didn't have many toys, which you'd have to have in a big city.

Town residents are aware of the negative urban imagery of small-town people as provincial, backward, and narrow-minded. Some town residents, as we shall see below, may reject being labeled a "small-town person" because the stigma of this imagery is a threat to their self-esteem. Town Folk, however, may directly challenge this imagery in defense of the self:

> I'm a small-town person. When I'm at work in Valley City, and I say where I live, people say, "That little hick town: You don't belong there. It's like a cowboy haven. There ought to be horses tied to posts instead of cars!" And I say, "Come on, we're not that backward." They have me living in Valley City: more sophisticated for some reason. They think they're more sophisticated when they live in bigger towns than when they live in smaller towns. It absolutely isn't true.... I don't think people are any more sophisticated in a small town or a city—I still think people are people.

Town Folk may even offer alternative interpretations of unfavorable images of small-town people, transforming purported liabilities into virtues. Though adopting the language of urban critics of the town, such a person may ironically declare that the "intolerance" of small-town people "really" represents a commitment to traditional small-town values:

> I would think I'm a small-town person. Perhaps I'm not as "broad-minded" as people who live in a larger city [chuckles]. Lots of people feel it's all right to drink if you don't become an alcoholic, but who knows when they're going to become an alcoholic? The people I know and the people I come in contact with—they don't believe that it's all right for people to do these things. Another issue that is coming to the fore is homosexuality. I don't think small-town people are as "broad-minded" [chuckles] concerning that as they are in the larger cities.

Country People

None of the individuals I spoke with reside on farms, ranches, or in the open countryside, nor are any directly employed in agricultural work. Yet, in Valleytown, more people described themselves as a "country person" than any other identity, and two residents of the suburban communities affiliated themselves with country life (see Table 3). On reflection, this serendipitous finding is less anomalous than it first appears. To many of Valleytown's *Country People*, Valleytown— as a "country town"—is *in* the country. Distinguishing simply between city life on the one hand and town and country life on the other, these individuals recognize no discrepancy between their community identity and their residential status. If the town could once symbolize urban ways in a more rural America, it is now conceived primarily as an element of rural life in the highly urbanized society of the late twentieth century (Strauss, 1961). Thus, a Country Person currently residing in suburban Bayside, remarks:

> Well, if I had my druthers, I'd be a small-town, country, or farm person. There isn't a lot of difference. They're all one kind: rural. I feel more comfortable there: I'm in my environment.

These Country People of town and suburb, however, also reemphasize the extent to which community identity must be interpreted as a symbolic construction. In a few cases, where Country People grew up on ranches or farms, this self-designation may mark a biographical reaffirmation of an agricultural past and an explicit affiliation with an agricultural way of life:

> I have things in common with other country people: I speak their language. I can speak the small-town or farm language. I know their hopes and their fears and their desires when they're talking about the price of grain. . . . When I lived in Montana, if a farmer or rancher or a sheep herder would come in, well, we'd hit it off right now. It's that feeling—you don't have to say it. How am I supposed to describe that? Well, they could say, "Doggone, that's a good rain we got," and I'd say, "Yah, now if she'd just quit for awhile so it wouldn't drown us out." Or, "the sun is sure burning us out." I understand what they mean—I can see the wheat curling over. I speak their language.

For most, however, this identity involves a diffuse commitment to rural, as *opposed* to urban, life—a commitment shaped by the traditional tenets of agrarian ideology in American culture: belief in the health and virtue of a simple life "close to nature," in the independence engendered by rural life, in the superiority of rural over urban life, and in the primacy of agriculture (Buttel and Flinn, 1975; Goldman and Dickens, 1983; Hofstadter, 1955). The nature of this affiliation is nicely reflected in the community preferences of Country People. Although relatively few Country People, when asked, chose a farm or ranch as the place where they would most prefer to live, *all* selected the city as the place where they would least like to live.[3]

How, then, do Country People use these images of rural life and people to construct an identity as a country person? Many begin by proposing that they are interested in nature and outdoor activities:

> I think of myself basically as a country person. I just enjoy being out in the country, in the outdoors, away from people and things. Enjoying the outdoors, whether it be the fresh air or going for a walk. I don't like being where there's lots of people.

In Hillcrest, a Country Person who grew up in rural Iowa but has now lived in the metropolitan area of San Francisco for more than fifty years expresses a more suburban version of this theme:

> I think of myself as a country person. I guess it's because of my background, because I was a country person as a child. I like things that are associated with it: I like gardening, I like horseback riding, I like walking.

For men, particularly, this self-image was often associated with outdoor sporting interests:

> I was born and raised in the country and that's the kind of living I like. I like the outdoors, the hunting, and the fishing.

Country People also propose that they are friendly and open. Unlike city people, Country People claim they will help out when needed, with no expectation of reward:

> I'm a country person: I feel better with cow shit on my boots [chuckles]. My mom taught me respect, loyalty, and sharing.

The guy who snubs you, if you give him time, he'll come
around. Be friendly, outspoken, and try to see things.
    [Do you think you have anything in common with other
Country People?]
    Giving, being friendly, if you need help, they'll help and
not ask for money. And you'll help them in return.

Though Country People pride themselves in their neighborliness and willingness to help others, they also suggest
that they are independent people who can "stand on their own
two feet." Thus, being a country person also involves a claim
to privacy and self-sufficiency. For a young man, this image of
"rugged individualism" may be exhibited in outdoor know-
how:

I'm a country person. I'm easygoing, quiet. I mind my own
business. I help other people when I can. . . . I can tell people
by the sound of their voice, whether they're country people
or a city person. City people talk faster. As a kid, I was in the
wilderness a lot. I learned how to take care of myself. Mostly,
up in the Sierras, around Shasta, but in the Rockies, too. If
you're in the wilderness, you can get along.

For a country woman, it manifests itself in interests in
crafts, "homemade" things, and "homespun" activities:

I like to think I'm a little more country, though I work in cities. I like making things, crocheting, canning, doing yard
work, hiking, fishing, training dogs. I ain't too much at keeping the house clean, like in the city, you have to for people
dropping in. I like woodcrafts, and my boy makes leather
things. Here you can encourage your kids to do things and
get involved. In the city, all they want to do is hang around on
street corners and go to shows.

This conception of independence and self-sufficiency is
also linked to a conception of Country People as more practical than city people. When asked about the influence of growing up in the country, Country People sometimes argue that
they have acquired a basic, well-rounded orientation to life. In
contrast to city people, who may be more educated, Country
People claim to possess more "common sense":

> It's more common sense that you pick up, more than any-
> thing else, growing up on a ranch. City kids have got a better
> education, but to apply it later, I think it's harder for them.
> They're very educated, very intellectual, but you get them out
> on a job . . . practical wise, they don't have the things we
> learned on a ranch: like we worked on equipment.

Unlike city people, who may excel in specific competen-
cies, rural life is thought to provide the individual with a
broad background of knowledge:

> Growing up on a ranch gives you a broad background. A per-
> son growing up in the city—maybe he knows a good deal
> about things I don't know about. But we were exposed to me-
> chanics—we took engines apart. The planting of crops and
> things that animals do, whether domestic or wild. We learned
> to drive early. When I went to college, I ran into people who
> didn't know how to cook or how to tune up their car. Maybe
> we were jacks-of-all-trades and masters of none, but we had a
> background where we could do just about anything.

This sense of identity—that being a country person involves a practical, all-around, down-to-earth orientation to
life—is also linked to egalitarian images of country people as
just "plain folks," ordinary Americans, without the preten-
sions or money of city people (see Vidich and Bensman, 1960):

> I'm a country person. You know, it's hard to take the country
> out of a boy. You can take the boy out of the country, but you
> can't take it out of the boy. I love to live in the country. I just
> feel, well, I just think it's kind of my class. I was never able to
> compete with the bigwigs in the town. I feel more at home.

Suburban Folk

In exploring the symbolic landscapes of community ideology, we saw that suburban ideology is less distinct, elaborate,
and salient than other community ideologies. Suburban enthusiasts, it is true, characterized suburbia in terms of the
American dream—of family and children, yard and home,
peace and security. Conversely, some urban critics of suburbia depicted an American nightmare—a place of homogeneity,
conformity, pettiness, sterility, and escapism. But for the ma-

jority of people with whom I spoke, suburbs and suburbia had relatively little meaning or significance.

This was true even in suburban Hillcrest and Bayside. Though suburban residents often expressed strong and complex beliefs about urban and small-town life, relatively few held comparable views on suburbia. Though they resided in communities that exhibit such popular, suburban iconography as California tract housing, cul-de-sacs, and swimming pools (Rapoport, 1982a), nearly half of those interviewed did not designate their community as a "suburb." With such an attenuated sense of suburbia, few suburban residents identified themselves as "suburbanites," and no interviewee living elsewhere claimed this designation.[4]

Those few individuals who do identify themselves as suburbanites—referred to below as *Suburban Folk*—draw upon the favorable cultural images of suburban ideology to describe suburbanites. They claim that suburban residents tend to be more concerned about family life, better educated, more well-to-do, more interested in their homes, schools, and community.

When questioned about their identity, they may nominally suggest that they are simply the kind of person who wishes to avoid the "crowdedness" of cities:

> I'm a suburbanite more than anything else. I don't like the crowds that much, and in a city, all we got is crowds. It's open in the suburbs, and I like that: it's compact, yet it's open.

... and who enjoys a place of escape from city life:

> I'm a suburbanite because I spend ninety-eight percent of my time here except for my job. This is where I live. My wife doesn't go anywhere and doesn't want to go anywhere, even though we do go some places.... I've grown accustomed to life in the suburb, and I like it. If you're away, you want to get back. If you're working some place in the city, you just have this great sense of relief to get away from the city and get back in suburbia.

Echoing the imagery of suburbia and the American dream, Suburban Folk may remark that they are more interested in home and yard, family and children, and, in some cases, community activity:

> Well, I would say I'm a suburbanite. I can't say I'm a small-town person, because my interests go way beyond Hillcrest, and yet, I don't want to live in a city if I can help it.
> [Do you think you have anything in common with other suburbanites?]
> Oh, yes. We all have our homes. And our children and our children's activities—their well-being. And our yards and gardens. The people we see and our friends have the same concerns.

Suburban Folk may even suggest that they are people of the "middle ground" (Donaldson, 1969; Marx, 1968), with qualities that draw on the best of city and small-town life:

> I think of myself as a suburbanite, if there is such a thing. I certainly don't think of myself as a city person or a country person. Maybe I just don't like crowds: there's a discomfort there. In a small town, there's just the opposite: I feel too sophisticated for a small town. There's a "ho hum" existence there. Maybe a bit of sophistication that you'd find in the city, but I'm more relaxed, more at ease.

But in general, suburban identity has relatively little significance to those who claim to be suburbanites, when compared to the community identities of City Folk, Town Folk, and Country People. Most residents of Hillcrest and Bayside believe that their communities are good places to live, but suburban ideology lacks sufficient meaning to construct a vital suburban identity.

Without Community Identity

Although eight out of ten contemporary Americans reside in a city, suburb, or town, some do not appropriate the imagery of community ideology to interpret their identity, nor do they express sentiments of affiliation with one form of community or another. How many people fall into this category is currently unknown, though in San Francisco, Hillcrest, Bayside, and Valleytown a significant minority of respondents did not affiliate with any type of community. These individuals, it is important to note, differ in the way they define their relationship to community; their differences also clarify community identity and its relation to community ideology.

Of those people without a community identity, some simply find community differences to be meaningless. This symbolic *placelessness* is similar to that described by Reed (1983) in his analysis of regional identity: southern residents who are relatively unaware of regional differences are less likely to identify with the South than those whose regional consciousness is high.[5]

This symbolic placelessness takes two forms. On the one hand, some individuals are minimally aware of the community landscape, including the form of community in which they reside. For example, in suburban Bayside and Hillcrest, where suburban ideology was quite attenuated, some residents had little sense of suburbs or suburbia:

> I don't really know the definition of a suburb—kind of out in the country—a bunch of houses out there. I don't really know.

Lacking the perspective and imagery of suburban ideology, these people did not "see" themselves as suburbanites:

> No, I don't [think of myself in terms of a community identity]; just an average person, nothing special.

> No, I don't think of myself as a suburbanite. People don't ask me that. They ask me where I live, and I tell them Bayside. I think of the name, not the suburb.

> No, [no identity]: I'm definitely not a city person: I hardly ever go to the city. And I don't want to live in the country. . . . I lived there three months in a little town, and I thought I was going to lose my mind. There was just nothing there. Lovely to visit, but I wanted more going on. So probably I want a small town near a city.

On the other hand, other individuals hold definite beliefs about communities but insist that forms of communities do not differ significantly. For instance, an elderly San Franciscan, troubled by the purported "decline" of public order in America, described cities, towns, and suburbs in the following manner:

> San Francisco's a typical city. Last year, I was back to Chicago, Buffalo, and Washington, and it seems to me that all the cities I visited—certain sections are deteriorating, same as they are here: the buildings, the commercial district, downtown.
>
> Small towns are not that much different from cities today, with transportation. They don't have plays and things, but they're not that handicapped. And there's problems with drugs and liquor and morality just as bad back in the Midwest [where I come from] as here. . . .
>
> Suburbs, I don't have too much sense about them. I feel people who move to the suburbs think they're going to get away from city problems—they want better schools, to get away from people. But they find the problems there too. My sister moved to Marin to get away from the blacks, but they've moved there, too.

Convinced of the uniformity of the community landscape, these people find the idea of community identity meaningless.

Other individuals do not identify with a form of community because they believe it is *inappropriate* for *them* to do so, even though they regard such identification as meaningful for others. Such *disaffiliation* can occur because an individual rejects potentially pejorative community imagery as stigmatizing. In Valleytown, as previously noted, some Town Folk actively challenge the negative characterizations of small-town people of urban ideology. Other town residents apparently reject the identity altogether:

> No, I don't think of myself that way [as a small-town person]. My husband and I were in Eastern Star and Shriners—we went a lot of places. So I don't feel real "hicky," if you know what I mean. And I think working in public—in the bank—helps a person an awful lot.

Other people reject a community identity because they conceive of themselves as particularly "adaptable"—people who "can live anywhere." *Adaptables* do recognize differences among places, but they argue that they "adjust easily." They

volunteer that they have developed the skills needed to live in
different types of communities by residing in various places.
Since they can "fit in anywhere," they minimize the significance of "where they live":

> I don't [identify with community], really, because I feel I
> could readily adjust to any of them if I wanted to. When I go
> to visit people who live other places, they say, "Oh, you look
> like a San Francisco person," . . . but I don't feel it.
>
> Where I live is not terribly important. I'm flexible to
> change, depending on the circumstances. But I think I'd have
> to weigh the advantages and disadvantages if I decided to
> move from here.

They may even reject the purported "virtues of rootedness," countering that a sense of community identity is
achieved only at the cost of boredom or provincialism:

> No, I don't think of myself that way [as a small-town or coun-
> try person] 'cause I am very easy to adapt. I can be with peo-
> ple who are very well educated, who are country folk,
> musicians, any type of people, and I can adapt myself to them
> and feel very much at ease. I've had to adapt to different sit-
> uations so it's not a problem at all. If somebody came and
> took this place and gave me a tent, I'd say, "Great!"—I know
> what that's all about. I know how to start a fire.
>
> I've moved a great deal. If I'd lived in one place, I think I'd
> have had a very dull life. It's very dull to sit in one place and
> never go anyplace.

Finally, some individuals reject a community identity because of a *divided sense of community identity.* Though we
have seen that some people retain a former identity that differs from the community in which they currently reside, others find such discrepant identity—and the symbolic conflict it
creates—more problematic:

> No, I don't [identify with a community]. I like to think of my-
> self as a city person, but I have the feeling I'm really a subur-
> banite. Because I like the positive things the city has to
> offer—and I use them, although you can tell, I don't have the
> nerve to put my family into some of the problems the city

also offers. So therefore, very sheepish, I guess, and that makes me a suburbanite, I guess, in actuality. But we use the city.

This divided sense of belonging—of ties to two places—was most salient and problematic when an individual, having grown up in and formed attachments to one type of community, moved to a different type under some constraint. For instance, years after following spouses from the city to the town, some women could express such conflict in community identity:

No, I guess I don't [identify with a type of community]. I guess what I am is a small-town person who likes to go to the city a lot. The trouble with a small town is that if you're interested in city things like the theater, you're stuck. I used to be so fond of the phrase "cultural vacuum," and that's the way I felt when we first got married and moved from the Bay Area [to Valleytown]. People thought I was a cultural snob.

Such people can recount, with considerable emotion, their troubled, costly, and incomplete transition from a city person to a small-town person:

I used to think of myself as a city person, and in a way sometimes I think I still do. A lot of being brought up in the city is still with me: I tend to maybe not to trust another person as much as someone here . . . and I love the city and love to go there. It's hard, but now, I really think I'm a bit of both—a small-town person and a city person. I could probably move back and fit right in.

When I moved to Valleytown, I hated it when I first came. Oh, God, I hated it. It was lonely. There were probably 3,000 people less than there is now. There was nothing downtown. I was used to being able to go downtown about anytime and get a coke or at least something. There's nothing to do. They roll up the streets at five o'clock. It took a lot of getting used to.

Community Identity and American Society

Residents of San Francisco, Hillcrest, Bayside, and Valleytown indicate that contemporary Americans think about their relation to community forms with more richness and complexity than is often assumed by scholars of modernity and identity (Figure 1). Some Americans readily designate themselves as a city person, suburbanite, small-town person, or country person. These people draw upon *community ideology* to articulate a *sense of belonging* to a form of community, an attachment based on varied ties of sentiment, interest, value, and knowledge. Such ties can be few and nominal, but in some cases they are clearly complex and rich, involving a substantial investment of self in place.

These people also present an *imagery of self* as a *type of person* with distinct qualities. City Folk talk about interests in culture and entertainment, and an open and liberal outlook; Town Folk say they are friendly, caring, and concerned with family, neighbor, and community. Country Folk note interests in outdoor recreation, crafts, and family life, and claim to be independent yet neighborly, commonsensical, and practical. Suburban Folk characterize themselves as people of the middle ground, desiring both the amenities of urban life and access to nature.

Other Americans do not use community forms as a locus or sign of identity. Yet these individuals are hardly alike. People with little sense of community differences find such identification meaningless (i.e., the Placeless); others reject such identification as stigmatizing or constraining (i.e., the Estranged and Adaptables); still others vacillate because of conflicting ties (i.e., The Divided).

This complex pattern of community identification suggests the need to revise the traditional sociological view of the decline of community in modern society and the growth of placelessness. True, American urbanization has transformed the spatial and social organization of locality during the last century and a half. Geographical mobility and mass institutions have altered the individual's relation to community and other forms of place. Yet the effects of these changes on community identity are not simple and must be studied rather than presumed.

Only one group—the Placeless—strongly supports the traditional critique of the decline of community and place identity in modern society. The fact that such placelessness was most commonly voiced in suburban communities may also reinforce this indictment. Suburbs have become the dominant residential form in late twentieth-century America and

Figure 1:
Community Identity: Self-Imagery by Self-Designation
and Community Ties

SELF-DESIGNATION
(Identity Types)

IDENTIFICATION WITH COMMUNITY:
TYPES OF TIES
(Sense of Belonging Varies—Nominal to Strong)

| | YES | | | | NO | | | NO/YES |
	City Person	Suburbanite	Small-Town Person	Country Person	Placeless (meaningless)	Estranged (stigmatizing)	Adaptable (constraining)	Divided (conflict)
sentiment	I love cities.	I like it: getting away.	I like towns.	I like country life.	—	—	—	I like towns but I also like cities.
interests	lots to do. theaters, restaurants, shopping. cultural activities.	home, children, things beyond here, too.	family, home, neighbors.	outdoors: hunting, nature. crafts.	—	—	different things.	city things and town things.
values/qualities	aware. liberal. open-minded. creative.	sophisticated but relaxed.	friendly. neighborly. religious. not permissive. not materialistic.	friendly. independent: own two feet. ordinary: practical, well-rounded.	just an average person.	not like that. not a hick.	adaptable can adjust to anywhere.	I'm a bit of both.
knowledge	how to act in city. how to get along.	about "things" beyond here.	about people here.	outdoor skills rural life.	places not different, important.	—	how to act in towns and cities.	—

are frequently criticized as relatively meaningless spaces
(Klapp, 1969; Packard, 1972; Relph, 1976).

However, notions of community decline certainly do not
fit well with those people who readily interpret themselves in
terms of community forms. City, Town, Suburban, and Country Folk do not simply reside *in* a place; they use community
ideology to articulate where they *belong* and *who* they are.
Nor does community decline aptly describe the dilemmas of
the Estranged and the Divided. If the Estranged reject an identity, they do so because such an identity seems stigmatizing,
not because communities have become meaningless. Their
hesitancy more likely reflects the conflicts of competing ideological interpretations than an erosion of meaning. If the Divided express conflict about "who they are," these conflicts,
again, suggest competing commitments to forms of community, commitments developed at different periods of their lives,
commitments grounded in different interpretations of community. Here, geographic mobility—and, particularly, involuntary
movement—may play a role in identity, but such mobility has
resulted in a conflict of meaning, not the loss of meaning pre-
dicted by the decline of community thesis.

Finally, the Adaptables are somewhat ambiguous in their
implications for our understanding of community, identity,
and modern American society. Adaptables, it is true, do not
feel they "belong" in any particular form of community; they
do not express the ties to place so readily volunteered by
those with traditional community identities. Yet they also
voice no regret about this state, and they regard their community "independence" as a virtue, an escape from constraint.
Rather than community decline, their identity may well point
to a new form of community identity, one grounded in mobility
and varied community experiences and skills, yet one appre-
ciative of the varied opportunities that different forms of community offer.

Part IV

Conclusion

Chapter 8

Community Ideology and American Culture

> People need to believe in the value of the com-
> munities in which they live, the goals they
> seek, and the satisfactions they receive.
>
> Maurice Stein,
> *The Eclipse of Community*, 1960.

Community Rhetoric and Values

In *Images of the American City*, Anselm Strauss (1961) proposes that much of the rhetoric of urban boosterism can be understood as an attempt by different cities to validate the claim that they are "authentic American communities." Despite the aura of factual debate that characteristically surrounds such discussion, Strauss contends that this interpretive process inherently involves matters of value. As city boosters select specific aspects of their city's life and history to present as distinguishing and exemplary characteristics, they relegate other less favorable features of community life to secondary status. In doing so, boosters incorporate implicit evaluations of the merits of different aspects of urban life into their community rhetoric, *selecting facts to fit taken-for-granted values*.

This evaluative process, Strauss suggests, works in even more subtle ways. If boosters are to substantiate their claims that their cities are *authentic* American communities, they must also *select values* they believe *will render the facts* of their community as quintessentially American. For example, city boosters in the West may identify their city with the fron-

tier, simultaneously declaring that frontier values and traditions are essential to American life. However, given the
diversity—and often contradictory structure—of American
values, boosters' claims of distinctively American values produce a collective babble of contradictory assertions. As a result, conflicts of "sectionalism versus national centralization,
of ruralism versus urbanism, of cosmopolitanism versus specialization, and of traditionalism versus modernism" are routinely reproduced in the community advocacy of urban
boosters (Strauss, 1961).

For instance, older cities maintain that their long history
ensures the cultivation of a distinguished, civilized way of life,
while younger cities present themselves as the rough and
ready embodiment of the spirit of American progress. Smaller
cities may stake their claim to authenticity on the fact that
they are the leading city of a region, while larger cities boast
that they have escaped the provincialism of sectionalism to
become national or even world cities. Such competing arguments climax in the varied rationale that different cities advance to capture the title of "most American city." New York
may claim this honor as the most dominant and diverse American city; Kansas City counters "as the crossroads and melting pot where the Southerner, the Northerner, the Easterner,
and the Westerner meet and become plain John American"
(Strauss, 1961).

Strauss's analysis of the reproduction of American values
in the symbolism of American urban boosterism provides two
important insights. First, the language of urban boosterism
necessarily employs an implicit *moral landscape.* Though
couched in a vocabulary of population size, urban growth, and
other mundane facts, this discourse at once accommodates
facts to values and selects values to render facts significant.
Second, Strauss's argument reveals how different—and often
contradictory—American values are used to legitimate community life. If New York becomes truly American by celebrating the diversity of ethnic cultures, Kansas City does so by
emphasizing the homogeneity of "plain John American." In
American culture, competing conceptions of *what communities ought to be* underlie the more manifest and mundane
claims of urban rhetoric.

A similar process is at work in the broader imageries of
urban, suburban, and small-town ideology. These competing

community ideologies effectively identify their way of life with the good life by incorporating contrasting conceptions of what communities *ought to be* into their language and perspectives. By emphasizing such divergent American values as simplicity and complexity, individualism and community, tradition and modernity, and the center and the periphery, community ideologies further legitimate the community interests and commitments of their adherents.

Community Ideology, Perspective, and American Culture

To explore how American cultural values are both incorporated in and expressed through community ideology, it will be useful first to reexamine the place and substance of community ideology in contemporary American culture. On the one hand, we have seen that the way contemporary Americans think and feel about cities, suburbs, and towns cannot be adequately understood simply in terms of their experiences with communities. Americans draw upon the cultural imagery of community life to interpret their experiences with places and, in doing so, they construct a sense of what communities are like that owes as much, if not more, to shared cultural resources as to personal experience.

On the other hand, we have seen that the community imagery of American culture, like a patchwork quilt, is not composed of a single fabric of cultural material. Rather, American culture incorporates different, contrasting community ideologies, each of which defines a distinct perspective on city, suburb, and town. Though Americans thus use cultural resources to interpret community life and experience, they do not draw upon a single, integrated system of community imagery, nor do they haphazardly adopt community images that drift, like particles of dust, in a free-floating cultural ambience. Instead, Americans with different community backgrounds learn dissimilar community ideologies that nourish distinct perspectives on community life. These ideological perspectives, thus, at once mediate people's relation *to American culture as a whole* as well as people's sense of community life as experienced in daily life.

As competing yet systemic interpretations of community life within American culture, community ideologies thus provide adherents with profoundly different conceptions of community life and community identity. Although no Villager, Urbanist, or Suburbanist articulates an ideology in its entirety, an enthusiast typically voices many of its tenets. Collectively, adherents thus come to share a community perspective that they both transmit and reinforce in the conversation of daily life. These competing perspectives can be briefly summarized in the following salient beliefs.

The Small-Town Perspective

—Small towns are quiet, easygoing places; cities are much too big and crowded, and they're dirty, noisy, and hectic.

—Small towns are neighborly: people are really friendly. Town folk have time for each other and help people in need. In cities, people don't even know who lives next door.

—Small towns are real communities. Everybody knows everybody in a small town. In cities, life is too impersonal and exclusive. City people tend to form themselves into cliques, where in towns everybody can join in.

—Small towns have more community spirit and moral vitality than cities. People who live, work, and play together are more concerned about their community. They want to know each other and to get involved with schools and other activities. City life is more transient. City people need to be entertained, and they are often too materialistic. Sometimes they are also self-centered and too competitive. All-in-all, small towns have not experienced the moral decline that cities have.

—Small towns are far safer places to live in than cities. People are basically honest in small towns, and they look out for each other. Cities are naturally dangerous places. They're so big and crowded that people get frustrated and commit crimes. Also, criminals are more tolerated in cities, and cities attract the kinds of people who are likely to get into trouble.

—Small towns are the best places for families and children. Small-town families stick together, and people are generally more family-oriented. Unlike city kids, small-town kids have plenty to do to keep them out of trouble, and there's lots of room to play, away from cars, concrete, and danger. And because everybody's interested in kids in a small town, it's easier to bring up your children on the right path.

The Urban Perspective

—Cities are really exciting places to live because they offer so much. Everything's happening in a city. With all the stores, people can find anything they want, and with so many theaters, sports events, and things like that, there is always something to do. In small towns, there's just nothing happening: they are a lot less stimulating places to live. Suburbs may be less boring than small towns because they're closer to cities, but cities are still better, because everything's right outside your door.

—Cities have all types of people, like America. Different groups live in different neighborhoods, and they all contribute something to the city as a whole. People in small towns tend to be just ordinary Americans, and suburbanites tend to be pretty much all the same—just family-type people.

—Cities are a lot more liberal than small towns or suburbs. With all the different things to do and kinds of people, city people are more aware of what's going on, and they're more tolerant, open-minded, and creative than small-town people or suburbanites.

—Cities offer more freedom than do towns or suburbs. City people have more opportunities for a good job, and with all the things to do and types of people, urbanites can live their life the way they want to. City people respect privacy, not like nosy small-town people or status-conscious neighbors in the suburbs. With their freedom, city people lead a happier life than do people elsewhere.

The Suburban Perspective

—Suburbs are close to the city, but they're nice, clean, and quiet, and they have more trees and grass than the crowded city.

—Suburbs are the best type of place because of home and family life. Suburbanites have a yard and a place of their own; they are not confined to an apartment like city people. Suburbanites keep up their property, and they're generally more interested in family life than are city people. Families do things together in the suburbs.

—Suburbs are ideal for kids. The schools are a lot better in suburbs than in cities or towns. You can protect your kids

from the city; but you can take them to cities for movies, mu-
seums, and things like that so they don't grow up totally isolated from everything like in a small town.

—Suburbs are pretty safe to live in—not like cities where
you can't live anymore. Suburbs are still interesting, though,
because they're close enough to the city that you can take advantage of the cultural opportunities. Unlike a town, you can
always go into the city for a night out.

—Suburbs are the best of both worlds. You're close
enough to the city without being mired down in all its problems. You have a nice, clean, safe community like a town, but
you're not entirely separated from the cultural advantages and
fun things to do in a city.

Community Perspectives and American Values

When directly juxtaposed, the community perspectives of
urban, suburban, and small-town ideology present striking
contrasts. These symbolic landscapes, we have seen, enable
Urbanists, Villagers, and Suburbanists to describe and explain
community differences in ways that legitimate community interests and commitments. They provide the symbolic framework for the articulation of a favorable and, in some cases,
complex sense of community identity.

This juxtaposition of perspectives also helps to clarify
how the rhetoric of community ideology at once incorporates
and expresses commitments to fundamentally different American values, values that further legitimate community interests. Like urban boosters who selectively adopt values to
authenticate their city as quintessentially American, community ideologies incorporate contrasting values from American
culture to identify their community with the good life. This
process is clearest in terms of urban and small-town ideology,
where Villagers and Urbanists imbue "similar facts" with profoundly different meanings by interpreting community life in
the context of divergent values.

First, though Villagers and Urbanists would both agree
that cities are more complex places than small towns, they
evaluate this difference in disparate ways (Figure 2). From the
perspective of small-town ideology, the *simplicity* of the town
is a virtue: it is order, immediacy, personal contact, and com-
prehensibility. Conversely, the *complexity* of city life—where

Figure 2:
Community Ideology as a Moral Perspective:
Simplicity Versus Complexity

Community Perspective

		Value	Landscape		Identity	
			Town	City	Town	City
C o m m u n i t y	Small Town	simplicity	small	big	normal	frustrated
				crowded		
			slow	hectic	easygoing	fast
			ordered	chaotic		mixed-up
			known	unknown		
			natural	dirty	outdoor	
I d e o l o g y	Urban	complexity	nothing	every-thing	naive	aware
				activities		active
			limiting	opportunity		
				diversity		
			boring	exciting		happier
			fragment	whole		
				real world		

everybody is "mixed together," where "nobody knows anybody," and where life is hectic—is conceived of as chaotic and
experienced as frustrating and alienating.

To the Urbanist, however, the complexity of the city is valued in its own right and also as the key to the good life. The
diversity of cultural, recreational, and commercial activities,
the variety of people, and the mosaic of neighborhoods that
the city provides—all create opportunities for individual fulfillment. Small towns and suburbs, in contrast, are not only
simple; they are too simple, too homogeneous, and, as a
result, too boring. Urban critics of town and suburb thus emphasize the limited opportunities of town life and the uniformity of suburban life.

Small-town and urban ideology similarly incorporate opposing evaluations of the value of *community* and the *individual* (Figure 3). Villagers celebrate the town as a communal
feast where human relations are personal, intimate, caring,
and where the social bonds of family, neighbor, friend, and
town still have permanence and meaning. Cities, conversely,
are thought to have lost their communal life. As a result, city
people are assumed to be more often isolated and lonely, and
the city person is portrayed as an individual who is often indifferent to the concerns of others at best and rude and exploitive at worst.

Although Urbanists may contend that urban neighborhoods do constitute miniature communities, they too identify
the city with the individual. They argue, however, that the individual in the city is the embodiment of personal freedom, a
freedom made possible by the complexity and diversity of city
life, urban respect for privacy, and urban openness and tolerance. Urbanists attribute communal relations to the town, but
they are likely to interpret small-town community as social
constraint: a place where gossip, pettiness, intolerance, and
personal oppressiveness are the norm. And when Urbanists
address suburbia, they may argue that the social uniformity of
suburbia also circumscribes individual freedom through conformity.

Both urban and small-town ideology assume that the
small town is a place of *conservatism* and *tradition* and that
the city is the home of *liberality* and *modernity* (Figure 4). Cities, Urbanists argue, ensure an awareness of diversity—a
grasp of the pluralism of American society. Such awareness,

Figure 3:
Community Ideology as a Moral Perspective:
Community Versus the Individual

Community Perspective

	Value	Landscape		Identity	
		Town	City	Town	City
Community Small Town	community	everybody knows everybody family real neighbors personal community spirit permanent	nobody knows anybody no place for kids impersonal transient	friendly family-oriented caring neighborly	(lonely) indifferent (rude) self-centered (rootless)
Ideology Urban	individual	constraint conformity	freedom your-own-thing privacy	gossipy ordinary narrow	more your-self interesting

Figure 4:
Community Ideology as a Moral Perspective:
Tradition versus Modernity

Community Perspective

	Value	Landscape			Identity		
		Town	City		Town	City	
Community							
Small Town	tradition	older way of life	decline		honest	aware	
		basic values	permissive		neighborly		permissive
			money and possessions				material-istic
			too competi-tive		caring		aggressive
Ideology							
Urban	modernity	behind the times	up to date		backward		aware
		very conserv-ative	liberal		narrow-minded		open
							creative
		tolerant	tolerant		(bigoted)		tolerant

they contend, produces a tolerance of people of different racial, ethnic, and social backgrounds, even encouraging an active appreciation of heterogeneity. Urbanists who identify with the city in turn claim that they are liberal, open-minded, aware.

Conversely, Urbanists depict the town as a place of conservatism and tradition. Portraying tradition as provincialism, they may contend that the town is not only an "older way of life" but also "backward" and "behind the times." Politically, small-town people may be described as not only conservative but too conservative—"right wingers," "extremists." Moreover, because the town lacks the social diversity of the city, small-town people—at best—are thought to lack an adequate understanding of the complexity of American life and to be less prepared to deal with the "real world." At worst, urban critics of the town may also assert that the simplicity of the town generates intolerance of others, noting that small-town people are "narrow-minded," bigoted, "red-necks." Similarly, Urbanists propose that suburbs, like towns, may breed prejudice and a "small-town mentality." To this charge, they may add that the very existence of suburbia—the home of "escapists" and "isolationists"—is grounded in racial intolerance.

Villagers, too, depict the town as the home of tradition and conservatism, but they maintain that small towns are places that have managed to conserve an older, better way of life. Small towns are places where traditional values of friendliness, neighborliness, and family have withstood the onslaught of change and where it is "still safe to walk down the street." Conversely, cities are rendered places not of liberality, but of moral decline and permissiveness.

Finally, both urban and small-town ideology place the town at the *periphery* of American life (Figure 5). Small towns are seen as locales not only geographically but also socially separated from the city, the locus of contemporary American life. To the Urbanist, the *centrality* of the city is a basis of opportunity, excitement, and being "where it's at," while the marginality of the town is symptomatic of provincialism, boredom, and lack of awareness.

Villagers also stress the separation of the town from the urban center of American life, although they may—when need arises—claim that small towns are "close enough" to the city. Seeing the city, however, as both the locus and symbol of the

Figure 5:
Community Ideology as a Moral Perspective:
Periphery versus the Center

		Community Perspective					
	Value	Landscape			Identity	
		Town	City		Town	City
Community Small Town	periphery	haven secure clean quiet	problems dangerous polluted noisy		easygoing	anxious (riff-raff)
Ideology Urban	center	provincial isolated small-time boring	where-it's-at access national exciting		out of it	involved knowledge- able

problems of contemporary American life, this separation is a virtue to Villagers. The small town is a haven of security—natural, quiet, free of crime.

Community Ideology as Moral Perspective

> If we perceive the debate over the question of community-society not as a scientific discussion of analytic theories but of the quality of contemporary life, our understanding of the terms is placed in a different context. It is not pertinent to ask if the past has *really* approximated the "community" or if the march of change leads straight on to "society." Rather, it is relevant to examine the present and adopt an attitude toward it.
>
> Joseph Gusfield,
> *Community: A Critical Response*, 1978.

In the concluding chapter of *Community: A Critical Response*, Joseph Gusfield asks why the concept of community has played such an important part in social theory, spanning the decades from Marx, Tonnies, and Durkheim to the present. He responds that this enduring role cannot be attributed simply to the utility of community as a scientific concept. Throughout much of his book, in fact, Gusfield criticizes the way social theorists have used the idea of community to analyze the change from traditional to modern society, a transition that has involved a movement from small to larger forms of territorial communities and, concomitantly, a purported shift from communal to more instrumental, rational, and segmental forms of human relations. Gusfield argues that this conceptual framework, embodied in contrasts of community and society, is scientifically inadequate as a *description* of human relations and social change. It does not depict human relations accurately either as they existed in the "little communities" of preindustrial society or in the urban, bureaucratic organization of modern life.

Gusfield then suggests that the enduring power of the concept of community must be found, not in its scientific utility, but in its "poetic" meanings: its power, as an expressive

metaphor and myth, to *evaluate* human relations. As a concept in social theory, community has also functioned symbolically as a utopia—an image of the past or future "about
which men and women are arguing." Social theorists might
place community—that utopian ideal of communal relations—
in the historical, lost world of the little community or in the
future society of a communitarian movement. But, he suggests, theories of community have always provided a foil to
human relations in the present, countering the purported inadequacy of current social ties as communal and fully-human
relations. Community, he thus implies, has always involved a
moral perspective, a symbolic posture that makes criticism of
human relations possible from the point of view of the communal ideal.

In this chapter, we have seen that the language of community in everyday life also involves implicit moral perspectives.
Popular ideologies of town, city, and suburb provide perspectives on daily life that do not simply describe what places are
like. In their imagery, language, and structure, they identify
one form of community with the good life, relegating other
forms to inferior modes of human association and social
identity.

We have also seen that the capacity of community ideologies to render different forms of community as ideal places is
based in part on the diverse, and often contradictory, structure of American values. If Urbanists, Villagers, and Suburbanists all believe that their communities are the best places to
live, they are able to do so in part because their ideological
perspectives are grounded in diverse and often opposing conceptions of what communities *ought* to be like. Small-town
ideology at once affirms the values of simplicity, community,
tradition, conservatism, and security, and it portrays the town
through an imagery that identifies the town with these values.
Urban ideology, conversely, both celebrates complexity, individuality, freedom, modernity, liberality, and it depicts the city
as source and locus of these virtues.

Suburban ideology also contributes to this interpretive
process, drawing on the competing values of city and town to
mark out its own moral ecology. Suburban ideology locates
the good life in the middle landscape, where "the best of both
worlds" come together. Selectively affiliating itself with city
and town, the suburban perspective "resolves" the contradic-

tions posed by the competing values of city and town. "Close to the city," suburban life is said to incorporate the opportunities, sophistication, and excitement of the city, avoiding the provincialism and boredom of the town. "Close to the town," it partakes in the serenity, security, and conservatism of the town, avoiding the noise, pollution, danger, and permissiveness of the city. Here suburbia mediates simplicity and complexity, community and the individual, tradition and modernity in the ideal of the middle landscape.

Such insights provide an important and final element to our understanding of the symbolism and workings of community ideology. Community ideologies not only describe and explain reality in profoundly "interested" ways; they infuse that reality—and our sense of ourselves—with significance, linking our conceptions of community life and identity to our most fundamental values as Americans. Such symbolic work suggests another reason for the persistence of community ideology in American culture. Community ideologies not only provide adherents with perspectives that affirm belief in a form of community life; they provide a language that enables contemporary Americans to symbolize, talk about, and to some extent resolve fundamental contradictions in American cultural values.

Appendix

Researching Community Ideology:
Reflections on Method

In his classic essay "On the Evolution of *Street Corner So-ciety*" (1955), William Foote Whyte describes the disjunction between serious social research as it is typically described in teaching and professional writing and "the actual process whereby research [is] carried out." Neither the selection of proper techniques nor the emergence of theoretical insight, he argues, takes place in a simple, straightforward manner. Rather, they occur, when they occur at all, with fits and starts, arising begrudgingly out of personal background and current experience, plodding analysis and flashes of insight, planned agenda and happenstance. Whyte's detailed account of his efforts to research and write *Street Corner Society* thus becomes a tale of contrast and change. He begins his work with a young man's interest in social reform and ends with a revolutionary interpretation of group process. He proposes a large-scale community study and completes a participant observation of the mundane, day-to-day activity of Doc and his gang. He works for a year and a half only to find his research given fundamentally new direction by realizing the deeper significance of bowling scores.

In this appendix I should like to describe some of the research process that led to *Commonplaces*. I do so as part of an ongoing dialogue that I have had with friends, mentors, colleagues, students, and manuscript reviewers who have inquired about "why and how I did what I did."[1] For the most part, this dialogue has been friendly, fueled by their curiosity and my desire to share the excitement of doing research. It also speaks to the uncertainty of the research process and the recognition of both the possibilities and pitfalls that such work entails.[2]

First Attempts: The Place Image Survey

Commonplaces began as a dissertation in sociology at the University of California, Berkeley. My interests in community belief and sentiment were quite diffuse, the product of a variety of sources rather than any single passion, experience, or theoretical agenda. To some extent, they were certainly an outgrowth of my community background, though I was only partially aware of this connection at the time. As I began work, I had lived in a wide variety of communities: small towns in Wisconsin, rural Vermont, and Kansas; mainline suburbs in metropolitan Chicago and New York; both small and large cities—Madison, Manhattan, Berkeley, and Oakland. I had, in fact, recently returned from a year's teaching in a small community on the shores of Lake Superior, and the contrast provided by this experience and life in Berkeley was dramatic. Such background nourished a general interest in community life and, I expect, an openness to exploring the diversity of community belief and sentiment.

At the same time, my interests extended direct intellectual concerns. From advanced study in both urban sociology and the sociology of culture (a somewhat unusual disciplinary combination), I was aware of radically disparate scholarship that had addressed community belief: social surveys on community preferences and satisfaction; highly refined interpretations of urban imagery in literary texts. I was both intrigued and annoyed by aspects of these traditions. Surely by "combining" the strengths of these approaches I could do "something creative" and produce original insight into community belief and sentiment.

With this basic agenda, I decided to undertake a social survey that would query contemporary Americans about community attitudes. I enlisted Claude Fischer and Charles Glock as advisors, both of whom were skilled in survey research design and analysis, and began work on a questionnaire and sample design. Using closed-ended questions, the first draft of the questionnaire addressed people's community preferences, their attitudes toward towns and cities, attitudes about community problems and related concerns (agrarianism, arcadianism, racism), community experience, and social background. The community attitude items were constructed from historical and ethnographic analysis of community imagery and represented a rather direct attempt to translate the insights of imagery studies to the world of survey research. Through this work, I hoped at once to analyze community preferences by situating them in a much more complex understanding of community attitudes and also to evaluate community imagery scholarship by assessing the actual use of images through empirical indicators and scales.

Over the next year, that questionnaire went through three major revisions. Some of these changes reflected shifts in emphasis and topic: I added questions on suburbs and suburbia to expand my coverage of community types. Most dramatically, however, the instrument evolved from a closed-ended questionnaire to a rather open-ended interview schedule. Through pretests of the questionnaire with friends and community residents, I became convinced that a structured dialogue with residents about communities would be more fruitful for a study of community belief and sentiment.

On the one hand, several problems with the questionnaire did not seem easily resolvable within the structured form. Although my community attitude questions would certainly provide some insight into people's posture toward communities, conversations with respondents suggested that people's views were more complex than these items implied. Moreover, basic assumptions about types of communities that I (and other community preference researchers) presumed and built into question wording did not seem to be shared by my respondents. The more I spoke with community residents, the more I developed the uneasy feeling that I needed to know much more about community belief and sentiment to write appropriate closed-ended questions. On the other hand, my pretest conversations with respondents convinced me that people had much to say on the topic, and that I needed to listen carefully to both their language and concerns. Rather than test for images through attitude items, I needed to let people talk. Their beliefs, in turn, could be treated as a text for interpretation; their language would provide a basis for inferring basic images of community life.

While I was working on the questionnaire, I constructed the design for the sample. My basic strategy was to develop a theoretically structured sample in which communities and neighborhoods would be selected to insure desired patterns of social variability and homogeneity, while individuals would be selected randomly from these target areas. Since community preference research indicated that community type was the single most important correlate of community preferences, I decided to select three communities in northern California that could serve as illustrative cases of a large central city, a metropolitan suburb, and a rural small town.

The selection of the three original communities—Valleytown, Bayside, and San Francisco—was guided by one major concern. While I knew that no single community could adequately "represent" the variety of communities of its type, I did want my sample communities to reproduce the differences of social ecology typically found among cities, suburbs, and towns in the United States. Specifically, this meant that I developed a list of fifteen potential communities in northern California; then used census data to compare each community to state and community norms for twenty-four selected social, economic, and demographic variables. In this way, I could ensure that the three communities differed from one another along significant dimensions (e.g., size, population growth or decline, social class composition, racial and ethnic heterogeneity, family status) and that such differences were those characteristically found among cities, suburbs, and towns. This material was supplemented with site visits to some suburban and rural communities, resulting in the selection of Valleytown, Bayside, and San Francisco.

Within each community, I decided to select neighborhoods to control the social composition of the sample and thus limit differences between communities due to respondent background. This seemed important particularly with respect to racial and class background, for preference work indicated that both were associated with broad community preferences. In the former case, the high racial and ethnic diversity of urban San Francisco, compared to the homogeneity of the suburban and small-town communities, prompted the decision to work in predominantly white, Anglo neighborhoods in San Francisco, hence controlling for racial background. With respect to social class, I believed it was possible to incorporate sufficient diversity within each community by carefully selecting enough neighborhoods in each community to achieve this end. Using data on census tracts and field observations, I thus chose three neighborhoods in Bayside and three in Valleytown that differed in the class composition of their residents. In San Francisco I selected neighborhoods that varied not only in class composition but also in their family status—that is, the proportion of families or single individuals in the area. As a result, the San Francisco interviews were drawn equally from five neighborhoods: an upper middle-class, family neighborhood; a lower middle-class, family neighborhood in the outer city; a working-class neighborhood; a traditionally working-class neighborhood undergoing gentrification with a highly mixed population; and an apartment neighborhood near the city center composed disproportionately of young, single, middle-class individuals.

Within this tiered framework of community and neighborhood variation, I selected individuals randomly. Within each neighborhood, I constructed a list of all households in two-to-four-block areas from direct observation of residences. Individual households then were selected on an interval basis, and where possible, respondent names were ascertained from mailboxes or a reverse telephone directory.

The Emerging Strategy

Work on the interview schedule and the sample, when coupled with ongoing reading and discussions, produced a clear thrust to my research by year's end. This direction was articulated in two documents: a formal dissertation prospectus and a research protocol for the Committee on Human Subjects at the University of California, Berkeley. In the former, "Talking Places: Community Perspectives in Contemporary American Culture," I proposed a study of community belief and sentiment based on qualitative interviews with people in Valleytown, Bayside, and San Francisco. I made a clear commitment to listen to people—to learn about their conceptions of community forms, their feelings about communities, their accounts of community differences, their sense of community identity. This was integrated with an explicit interest in community perspectives: "[the work will] move toward a cultural depiction of community perspectives, trying to identify the typical ways which Americans (and groups of Americans) use the symbolic resources of contemporary culture to interpret the meaning of community." Yet, in this thirty-five page document, I made little mention of community ideology, only intimations of "styles of thought" and perspectives that involve ties to place.

For the next year, my work focused primarily on interviewing, using a fifth version of the schedule. This schedule worked quite well, and was modified only once more, primarily for question order (see Exhibit A). The organization of topics and question format now proceeded generally along three lines. First, the earlier sections of the interview focused on the respondent's beliefs about specific places rather than different forms of communities. These questions (for example, about the person's childhood residence) enabled the respondent to speak easily and openly about communities and for me to listen, indirectly, to their designations and characterizations of forms of communities. Second, earlier sections of the interview emphasized descriptions of communities, while later sections asked for more explicit evaluations and interpretations of communities (for instance, community preferences). This facilitated a direct assessment of the individual's imagery and sense of community landscape before directly addressing deeper feelings and commitments. Finally, early questions were the most open-ended, while concluding questions were more focused. This strategy permitted all respondents to communicate their particular sense of community life; yet enabled me to ask all respondents directly about certain aspects of community life that I deemed significant.

The sample, as designed, proved fruitful yet difficult in two ways. First, with the completion of half of the interviews, analysis of the social composition of respondents indicated that most of the respondents from Bayside were from working-class households. (Typically, the husband worked in a skilled or semiskilled blue-collar job, while the wife worked part-time in low-level white-collar employment.) To insure sufficient class diversity, I thus added upper middle-class Hillcrest to the sample, again specifying two neighborhoods and listing households.

Second, locating and gaining consent from potential respondents was an arduous though not impossible process.

Exhibit A
Commonplaces: Interview Schedule

The following outline of topics summarizes the substance and order of questions used in the sixth and final draft of the interview. The actual schedule, with complete question texts and space for notes, ran 26 pages. For several important questions, I have included the actual text. Important probes are indicated in brackets.

I. Cover Page

    A. Respondent code: location in sample
    B. Introduction to interview

II. Community Background: Beliefs about Specific Places

    A. Childhood community(ies)
       • description
       • feelings
    B. Previous community
       • description
       • reasons for moving
    C. Current community
       • description as particular place
       • feelings about moving

III. Beliefs about Forms of Community

    A. Forms of community: community of residence
       • typicality of current community as form of community (their classification)
       • description of form

          Question text: Suppose you had a relative who'd never lived in a (PRESENT COMMUNITY TYPE) and who was about to move to a (SAME). If he or she wrote you and asked you what (SAME) are like in general, what would you respond? [people, life?]

    B. Other forms of community
       • designation of other forms (develop types from Part II)
       • description of other forms [remaining two major types—city, small town, or suburb]
       • example of a typical (city, suburb, small town)

IV. Community Preferences and Identity

    A. Community preferences
       • particular ideal place

• form of ideal community; form of least preferred community

> Question text: Card A lists a number of different types of places—a city, suburb, a small town, a farm, the countryside, and the wilderness. Suppose you had to choose a place to live on the basis of whether it was a city, a small town, a suburb, or some other place on this list. If you could live anywhere you wanted, what type of place would you most like to live in? [(If a small town, a farm, the countryside, or wilderness): How many miles would you like your community to be from a city?]

B. Community identity
  • self-characterization as community form

> Question text: Do you think of yourself as a city person, a small-town person, a suburbanite, or a country person, or don't you think of yourself in such terms? [(IF YES): How do you see yourself? Things in common with others? Always thought of yourself as a (identity)?]

  • home—particular community? [other special communities?]
  • sense of mobility

V. Community Issues

Where not adequately covered in Parts II–IV, directly ask to evaluate and interpret certain issues.

A. Friendliness and community life
B. Environment (dirt/pollution)
C. Crime and safety
D. Children and community

VI. Social Background and Community Activity

A. Demographic background
B. Community involvement
C. Mobility and commuting

VII. Field Notes

A. Respondent's housing
B. Interview interaction and tape key
C. General comments

The very strengths of the sample—its diverse community and neighborhood structure—clearly exacerbated the process of simply making contact with people. As a solitary, unfunded interviewer, I regularly visited thirteen neighborhoods in four communities in a 110-mile radius of Berkeley. Moreover, by randomly selecting individuals, rather than basing selection partially on respondent referrals, I increased the likelihood of possible respondent rejection. To counter these difficulties, I sent a letter of introduction several days before visiting a household for the first time (Exhibit B) and left follow-up notes to people who were not home. This tactic, coupled with persistence (up to four return visits for people not at home), resulted in in-depth interviews with more than half the people contacted. Review of those individuals who declined to be interviewed suggested that they did not differ greatly in social background from people who accepted, and the final sample included much of the structured community and social diversity I desired (Table 4).

The interview experience itself proved both valuable and exciting. In most cases, people enjoyed talking about communities, and interest in the topic surely facilitated establishing rapport with respondents. In all cases, I made notes as the interview progressed, and in all but a small number of cases, people consented to simultaneous recording of our dialogue. The interview typically lasted an hour to an hour and a half, but in some cases, it ran over two hours.

Analysis and Community Ideology

Though interviewing continued into the third year of work, the process of analysis was well underway by this time. To some extent, this was the inevitable outcome of simply processing the information I was generating. Typing transcripts of interviews, deciphering interview notes, developing summaries of respondent orientations—all forced a continual interaction with the data and a growing awareness of simple patterns in the welter of information. My procedure of doing small batches of interviews in one community, moving to another, then returning to the first for another batch, also sensitized me to the variety of voices I was hearing in different community contexts.

Table 4: Characteristics of Sample by Place of Residence

	San Francisco	Hillcrest and Bayside	Valley-town	Total
*Length of Residence**				
less than one year	12	15	4	10 (8)
1 to 4	16	35	32	27 (21)
5 to 9	15	23	16	18 (14)
10 to 19	12	15	24	17 (13)
20 to 39	30	12	12	18 (14)
40 + years	16	0	12	9 (7)
	101%	100%	100%	99%
	(26)	(26)	(25)	(77)
Age				
18–29	23	15	16	18 (14)
30–49	43	58	40	47 (36)
50–69	27	15	32	24 (19)
70 +	8	12	12	10 (8)
	101%	100%	100%	99%
	(26)	(26)	(25)	(77)
Gender				
women	38	50	60	49 (38)
men	62	50	40	51 (39)
	100%	100%	100%	100%
	(26)	(26)	(25)	(77)
Marital Status				
married	35	65	60	53 (41)
divorced	27	4	20	17 (13)
widow(er)	8	4	12	8 (6)
separated	4	8	4	5 (4)
never married	19	15	4	13 (10)
living together	8	4	0	4 (3)
	101%	100%	100%	100%
	(26)	(26)	(25)	(77)

Table 4: (Continued)

	San Francisco	Hillcrest and Bayside	Valley-town	Total
Length of Education				
11 years or less	8	0	20	9 (7)
12	27	23	44	31 (24)
13–15	19	42	20	27 (21)
16 or more	46	35	16	33 (25)
	100%	100%	100%	100%
	(26)	(26)	(25)	(77)
Occupation: Head of Household				
white collar upper	31	54	28	38 (29)
lower	31	15	16	21 (16)
blue collar skilled	19	19	12	17 (13)
semiskilled	15	8	36	19 (15)
unskilled	4	4	0	3 (2)
farm	0	0	8	3 (2)
	100%	100%	100%	101%
	(26)	(26)	(25)	(77)
Family Income				
less than $8,000	15	4	28	16 (12)
8–15,000	38	19	12	23 (18)
16–23,000	15	27	44	29 (22)
24–31,000	19	23	8	17 (13)
32–39,000	0	8	4	4 (3)
$40,000 or more	8	15	0	8 (6)
not ascertained	4	4	4	4 (3)
	99%	100%	100%	101%
	(26)	(26)	(25)	(77)

*Length of residence includes multiple stays in a community. Residents of San Francisco and Valleytown are more likely to have lived more than once in their current community.

Exhibit B
Letter Sent to Prospective Respondents:
San Franscisco Version

Dear (NAME, IF POSSIBLE):

I am writing to invite you to participate in a study designed to learn how Americans feel about the communites in which they live. This study is being carried out as a doctoral research project at the University of California under the direction of Dr. Claude Fischer.

I would like, if you will agree, to interview you about your feelings about San Francisco, other communities you've lived in, and places in general. I think you will enjoy the interview. Moreover, your participation in this project will help the public and city planners to make wiser decisions about the future of American communities.

Your interview will be confidential, and it will be reported, along with others, in general terms so that no individual or small community can be identified. During the interview, I will take notes, or if you prefer, I will record the interview. While I am confident you will want to complete the interview, you may, if you wish, withdraw at any time.

Within a week I will call on you in person to arrange a convenient time to talk with you or some other member of your household. If you have any questions about this study, please feel free to contact me by letter or telephone (call collect: 843–1310).

Thank you for your cooperation.

Cordially,

David M. Hummon, M.A.
Community Perspectives Project

Claude Fischer, Ph.D.
Department of Sociology

P.S. You may be wondering how you were chosen to participate in this study. Your household was selected as a part of a carefully chosen sample of households in several communities, a sample designed to insure the participation of a wide variety of people. With everyone's participation, this design will insure an accurate picture of how Americans feel about places.

My first attempts at analysis moved in two directions, both of which were necessary yet ultimately tangential to the final argument. First, following the lines of preference research, I was interested in assessing the social correlates of individual community preferences in my sample. To some extent, this was motivated by a desire to substantiate the validity of the sample. Thus, I compared the preference patterns of my respondents to random samples of larger populations. For example, using unpublished data from Claude Fischer's Northern California Community Study, I was able to substantiate that the community preferences expressed by residents of my communities were similar in direction and rates to those of northern California communities, and that these, in turn, were similar to those of the country as a whole (see Table 5).[3] This work was also important in reemphasizing that community itself was the most important social correlate of community preference in my sample. Though residents of a single place were far from unanimous in their preferences, community, rather than class or gender, did appear to be most directly associated with the orientations expressed by my respondents.

Second, following my interest in community imagery, I began to analyze the beliefs used to describe forms of communities. Beginning with the small town, I used respondent descriptions of towns, town life, and small-town people to

Table 5: Community Preferences by Community:
Northern California Communities*

Community Preference	Central City	Inner Suburb	Community Outer Suburb	Small City	Small Town
Large city	41	9	9	5	7
Small city	22	26	11	21	11
Suburb	11	18	22	6	4
Small town	8	21	24	39	47
Farm/rural	18	27	34	29	31
Total	100%	101%	100%	100%	100%

*Northern California Community Study, Claude Fischer, Principal Investigator, unpublished data. These data are based on a random, stratified (by place) sample of 1,050 northern Californians. The survey was conducted in 1977.

build an exhaustive summary of beliefs expressed in the interviews. This material documented the wide range of beliefs that Americans could use to characterize town life, and clearly substantiated the range of meanings that communities might have for individuals. When coupled with analysis of the community background of individuals, this work suggested how community background might shape community preferences through socialization to a community imagery. In this vein, I wrote an essay on the small-town imagery of small-town and metropolitan Americans and proceeded to an analysis of urban imagery.

At this point, I began to rethink my work significantly and to move to an explicit analysis of community ideology. Though this change took place gradually, it emerged from a growing awareness of the conceptual power that community perspectives offered for understanding my interviews. Hence, although analysis of the collective imagery of small towns, cities, and suburbs suggested that each form of community connoted a wide range of meanings, beliefs about one form of community for any individual were clearly linked to beliefs about other forms of community life. Within a diversity of imageries, individuals voiced patterns of community landscapes, patterns that were apparent only if you examined how people thought about all forms of communities rather than their attitudes toward a single locale. Analysis of an individual's perspective on communities—with its emphasis on *systems* of imagery and meaning—seemed to provide a more economical and accurate characterization of contemporary community beliefs.

At the same time, reanalysis of the interviews indicated these individual perspectives on communities were shared perspectives. This was clearest in Valleytown, where the town as an ideological context provided a collective view of what communities are and ought to be like. In this context, it was easiest to conceive of a community perspective as part of a shared tradition rather than a simple "outgrowth" of individual experience and to move away from the individualistic assumptions of much community preference research. Now the association of community residence and community preferences "made sense," but it did so within a growing understanding of the extent to which individual views were grounded in shared perspectives on the community landscape, perspectives that were situated within alternative community ideologies.

Afterthoughts and Beyond

The journey from an awareness of the importance of community perspectives and ideology to the completed analysis of *Commonplaces* is long. It involved more analysis of the data, a conceptual linking of accounts, identities, and values to the symbolic work of community ideologies, and an articulation of the place of these ideologies in American culture. Yet this critical activity comes after most of the research process was completed and thus falls beyond the scope of these reflections.

With hindsight, it is easy to see strengths and weaknesses in the research process, some of which are all too apparent in the twists and turns of my adventure into the "real world." Three deserve specific comment, though, for they suggest both possible mistakes to be avoided and new directions for further work.

First, my concern for the design of the sample at the level of the community and individual was well founded in one sense. The comparative framework was critical to systematic comparison of community belief and consequentially essential to an emerging sense of community ideologies. Yet in retrospect some aspects of this emphasis seem misplaced. Though my attempt to insure that my sample communities were socially representative of their community forms was appropriate, I may well have overestimated its importance, incorrectly assuming that community beliefs are a relatively direct product of community experiences. To the extent that community perspectives are appropriated from cultural ideologies, the representativeness of communities and community experiences may well be less critical for community perspectives than I assumed.[4]

Similarly, my concern with the social composition of communities was worthwhile: by controlling for group differences through neighborhood selection, I was able to highlight differences associated with community background. The sample, however, might well have been generated more efficiently, with fewer problems of respondent rejections, by asking some re-

spondents for a single referral to other community residents
with selected social characteristics.[5] In the latter stages of the
interview process, I might also have actively pursued individuals with strong commitments to different types of places to
insure a rich characterization of these community perspectives. The sample, as designed, certainly generated such community enthusiasts in city and town, but it was considerably
weaker in this respect in the suburban communities.

Second, though my primary focus on beliefs about forms
of community rather than particular communities was fruitful, it seems somewhat overdrawn in retrospect. (At the time,
this theoretical direction was reinforced by the request of the
Committee on Human Subjects at Berkeley to protect the anonymity of the smaller communities.) Yet, by excluding the
identity—and hence the particularity—of places, I undoubtedly lost avenues of inquiry important to a broader cultural
analysis of community ideology and identity.

For instance, some communities unquestionably sustain
local cultures that defend particular community identities.
These local ideologies deserve serious attention in their own
right, and they inevitably become part of the dialogue about
community life of broader community ideologies.[6] Moreover,
this exclusion also made it unlikely that I would directly assess the relation of community ideology to the everyday interpretation of the built environment of communities. Particular
elements of physical environment undoubtedly serve as public symbols or icons of the community, serving both to communicate the identity of the community as a particular locale
and as a form of community. Lacking a serious focus on the
particular place, however, I did not examine the meanings that
such community iconography might convey for community
ideology, nor did I directly assess the degree to which individuals "read" the physical landscape in terms of community
ideology.[7]

Finally, though I originally included questions on community politics and policy in my original questionnaire, these
items were dropped as I moved to a more unstructured format.
That they did not reemerge in the interviews suggests the substantial degree to which contemporary Americans, in drawing
on community ideology, do *not* conceive of the fundamental
qualities of community life as a product of the political process. My analysis of community accounts suggests that the

rhetoric of community ideology, in fact, reinforces a "depoliti-cized" view of the sources of and solutions to community problems.

Nevertheless, I suspect, though I cannot show, that con-temporary Americans, when involved in community move-ments or local politics, do draw upon community ideologies to legitimate their commitments and political action. As an ur-ban social movement, the efforts of gays to construct a dis-tinct gay community within San Francisco during the 1960s and 1970s provide an excellent case in point (Castells, 1983). Urban ideology, with its emphasis on diversity and opportu-nity, liberality and personal freedom, and creativity and spon-taneity, may well have provided an effective rhetoric for legitimating the spatial and political claims of gays and for af-firming and celebrating the distinct public culture of the gay urban community. Such appropriation of community ideolo-gies for political discourse and action surely occurs in other community conflicts, both at the local level (e.g., growth poli-tics in suburb and small town) and at the national level (e.g., federal urban policy). As such, this process deserves serious study to enrich our understanding of both community con-flicts and the symbolic work of community ideology.

Notes

Chapter One: Community Perspectives

1. The town clearly remains a significant symbolic locale in the post-World War II fiction of writers like Cheever and Updike. In more popular works, it is central to the presentation of the American experience, spanning the decades from Metalious's *Peyton Place* (1956) and Norman Rockwell's Stockbridge in the 1950s to the *Blue Highways* of William Least Heat Moon (1982) and Garrison Keillor's *Lake Wobegon Days* (1985) in the 1980s. For other discussions of the town in American literature, see Goist (1977) and Lingeman (1980).

2. See Freidel (1963) and Strauss (1961) for accounts of the history of American boosterism; Meinig (1979), for historical changes in the "ideal community" in American society. Tuan (1974) argues that city-boosting has produced a particularly rich vocabulary of urban identities in American society. He describes how such names change historically and how they are used to symbolize various facets of a city's reputation. Chicago, for instance, was once the Garden City; more recently it has been the City by the Lake, Hogopolis, the City of Big Shoulders, the Windy City, and the Crime Capital.

3. Children's books are a rich repository of community ideology. Though no one has systematically analyzed these texts in this light, it appears that American children's literature was dominantly "antiurban" until well into the 1960s. For example, Virginia Lee Burton's (1942) *The Little House* tells the story of the deterioration and desertion of a house as it is incorporated into the expanding city—and of its renewal as it is literally moved back to the countryside. Recently, a more favorable literature of the cities has emerged, apparently responding in part to the vocal demands of urban (often minority) residents and educators for a usable literature. Like Sesame Street on TV, books now portray urban streets, neighborhoods, and apartment life as a normal, and admirable, part of American life.

4. The community imagery of popular culture has received some attention. See, for instance, Nachbar (1983) for a treatment of place imagery in 19th-century Currier and Ives prints; Lohof (1983) for an analysis of the frontier individualism of Marlboro cigarettes; Hummon (1988) for urban imagery in contemporary tourist advertising; Francaviglia (1976) for Walt Disney's rendition of small-town America. Fischer (1984) and Furay (1977) also provide useful examples of urban and small-town imagery in popular culture.

5. Judith Martin's (1979) advice on "The Virtuous Life in the Wicked City" follows a long-standing tradition. When cities and urban life were new to many Americans at the turn of the century, such advice on proper urban behavior was a regular feature of etiquette books. On this topic, and other aspects of urban learning, see Lofland (1973).

6. There is virtually no comparative cross-cultural work on community ideology. Fischer (1984) contains simple data on community preferences in France and the United States. Schorske (1968) examines conceptions of urban life among 18th- and 19th-century European intellectuals, noting the particularly favorable view of city life of the French Enlightenment. Williams (1973) provides an insightful historical analysis of the interaction of class and community ideology in the literature of England; Marcus (1975), an interpretation of the changing conceptions of city life in Victorian England and Engel's depiction of Manchester.

Chapter Two: Minding Community

1. For instance, see Strauss's (1968) excellent use of novels depicting New York City as a vehicle for identifying broader urban images in American culture.

2. In some cases, verbal information about places is collected, then transformed into spatial form by the researcher. See Gould and White (1986), for instance, for the transformation of spatial preferences into spatial form. Tuan (1977) has critically argued that mental map research, based on people's sketch maps, captures a very limited sense of people's subjective experience of place because it relies on relatively sophisticated conceptual skills.

3. Rapoport (1982a) and Zeisel (1973, 1984) provide critical discussions of the way professional designers frequently evaluate the built environment differently from people who reside in these environments.

4. See Marans and Rodgers (1975) for an excellent review of the role of community satisfaction studies in quality of life research; Guest and Lee (1983) for a summary of the current status of this work. As the latter note, the results of this work are difficult to summarize because of the widely discrepant samples, variations in measures, and less than consistent attention to the role of the environment as subjectively perceived by the respondent or as independently measured by the researcher.

5. Respondents were asked to rate their community of residence on a seven-point satisfaction scale: 34% said they were completely satisfied (rating 1), 78% said they were "satisfied" (ratings 1–3).

6. Evidence on the social correlates of community satisfaction is most consistent for differences of race and age; less so for social class and length of residence. For instance, Marans and Rodgers (1975) report a small, inverse relation between class (as measured by income) and satisfaction.

7. This is not to say that other disciplines have not contributed to this literature. The work of social and phenomenological geographers is also notable in this context: Tuan (1974, 1977, 1980), Buttimer (1980), and Seamon (1979).

8. See Fischer (1977), Gusfield (1978), Hunter (1978), and Nisbet (1969) for more extended discussions of the "decline of community thesis" in classic sociological theory. Harvey (1985b) extends the Marxist analysis of the corrosive power of money and markets on places, a power that transforms particular and meaningful places into the abstract spaces of commodities.

9. This work typically emphasizes the "extrinsic" character of knowledge about places. Sociologists have generally been most interested in symbols that are socially sustained by shared beliefs of local subcultures (see Suttles 1972, 1984). Designers and geographers have examined more closely how the built environment itself is imbued with meaning and becomes a mnemonic for social communication (Rapoport, 1982a; Duncan, 1973, 1982), but see also Lofland (forthcoming).

10. Harvey (1985b) notes that this ideological convergence of interests of community integration and economic boosting always involves an uneasy tension. Ultimately, the interests of capital, in which places are arenas for the search for profit, do not coincide with the particularistic loyalties of places as communities. Community loyalties, whether to neighborhoods or the city as a whole, thus have the potential to counter the forces of capital through antigrowth politics and other urban protest movements (Castells, 1983).

11. Krase (1979) presents an interesting case study of such a stigmatized neighborhood and the efforts by community activists to overcome identity assault. Little systematic work directly documents the notion of stigmatized places. The popular press provides various examples of both public debates and private feelings over stigmatized places. See, for instance, an article describing the elimination of the name of an historical black community called "Nigger Heaven" from public maps and documents (Milich, 1987), or Howard's (1986) discussion of her troubled feelings about "being from" the old industrial port of Bridgeport, Connecticut.

12. Broader social statuses were also associated to some extent with such knowledge: white residents and those of higher social class tended to be more knowledgeable. Patterns of activity—where one shopped and worked—were not. Guest and Lee (1983) also present some evidence that suggests that the structure of the built environment (e.g., the presence of parks) is of importance to such recognition, consistent with work on mental maps. These findings, however, are somewhat ambiguous, as such landmarks may function primarily as *symbols* within a context of local culture.

13. Commentators and scholars disagree significantly on the sources of such antiurbanism. Some writers tend to treat such antiurban preferences as a simple, direct reflection of urban life (Campbell, 1981). Others suggest that its sources are more complex, rooted in the relatively recent transition of American society from a rural to an urban society (Kristol, 1970) and a long standing antiurban bias of American culture (Blackwood and Carpenter, 1978).

14. Warner notes that the 19th-century poor did not see themselves as living in "a slum." Ethnic Italians, living in Boston's West End in the 1950s, similarly did not conceive of their neighborhood as a "slum" on the eve of its destruction for "urban renewal" (Gans, 1962).

15. Community ideology, it is worth noting, may also be seen as one particular type of place ideology, where a place ideology is any system of belief that uses locality and its properties to interpret social reality and that does so in an argumentative and justificatory manner. Other types of place ideologies include regional ideologies— to wit, claims of southern hospitality, New England integrity, midwestern "Americanness," Western individualism—and local, booster ideologies of particular neighborhoods and communities. See, for instance, Cuba (1987), Reed (1983), Tuan (1974, 1977), Strauss (1961), and Suttles (1984) for examples of such boosterism at the regional and local levels.

16. None is highly atypical, either. Despite popular images of the deviant character of life in northern California, Fischer (1982) pre-

sents considerable evidence that such regional stereotypes are exaggerated. Even San Francisco, which claims to be "Everybody's Favorite City," is not as atypical of American cities as the Chamber of Commerce would contend in terms of its residents, economy, or institutional problems (see Wirt, 1974). To the extent that San Francisco is unusual in sustaining a relatively high quality of urban life in the 1970s and 1980s (Castells, 1983), it provides an excellent place to locate urban enthusiasts. For a more extended discussion of the selection of both communities and respondents, see the Appendix.

17. For example, in 1970 approximately 11% of California residents were blacks or members of other racial minorities. Of San Francisco residents, 29% were minority members, and nearly 11% were of Spanish descent. In contrast, blacks and other racial minorities composed 1% of the population of Hillcrest, 3% of Bayside, and 4% of Valleytown. It would, of course, have been possible to choose suburban and small rural communities with substantial proportions of minority members. This, however, creates another problem for a small, comparative case study: given the residential segregation of American communities, particularly for blacks, such communities are quite atypical.

18. A brief summary of the social composition of the sample is included in the Appendix, Table 4. The sample, of course, lacks any regional variation. National preference studies, however, indicate only small and contradictory differences in the community preferences of people living in different regions of the country. It appears to be the case that residents of the south and midwest are most antiurban; those of the east and to a lesser extent west are less antiurban.

Chapter Three: Small-Town Ideology

1. Sections of this chapter were previously published in "Popular Images of the American Small Town," *Landscape*, 24, 2 (1980): 3–9, and are reprinted with permission of the publisher.

2. For instance, see also the special issue of *Newsweek* devoted to "The Small-town Boom" (July 6, 1981).

3. For scholarly discussions of nonmetropolitan growth and the small-town revival, see DeJong and Sell (1977), Blakely and Bradshaw (1980), and Hawley and Mazie (1981).

4. The 90% figure is based on a special survey conducted by Gallup in November 1976. The poll seriously inflates the nonmetropolitan response by omitting suburbs as a possible response category.

The reported percentages were 13% large city; 29% small city; 20% small town; 38% rural America.

5. This tendency to substitute psychological motives for the interpretation of symbol systems has been common in the social sciences and popular press. Geertz (1973) presents a cogent theoretical critique of this process. See also Wright (1975) for a similar argument and a structural explanation of the popularity of the western movie that goes beyond the imputation of motives.

6. These unpublished data are from the Northern California Community Study, Claude Fischer, principal investigator. The estimates are based on a random stratified (by place) sample of 1,050 northern Californians in 1977. For the complete table of community preferences, see the "Appendix," Table 5.

7. This fact was first encountered as a "methodological problem" in the early stages of the research. Armed with a battery of survey questions, discretely arranged by community and topic, I found in pretesting that the people I interviewed would not "stick to the schedule of questions." I was, at first, quite annoyed by this, as I had spent considerable time developing a formal questionnaire. After reflection, I realized that my logic—based on the analytic categories of sociological analysis—was hardly theirs and that this difference was crucial. This recognition, along with problems with preference questions and other items, led to a reorganization of the interview process and to a considerably different study. See Rabinow's (1977) extended reflections, based on his field work in Morocco, on the importance of such methodological disruptions to the study of culture.

8. The town simply has too many residents for everyone to be acquainted with everyone else. Moreover, town life, as Vidich and Bensman (1960) argued, is differentiated along lines of class, age, and gender so that residents are much more likely to interact and know some residents more than others.

9. "Centrality" is a wonderfully flexible notion. Residents of all four communities were able to place their community "in the center" by selectively choosing places "on the periphery."

10. Both Goist (1977) and Smith (1966) analyze the favorable image of the town in early twentieth-century literature, including the work of Zona Gale.

11. Sinclair Lewis's *Main Street* (1920), the best-known work, was the nation's best selling novel in 1921 (Hackett and Burke, 1977). Unlike the heroine of Dreiser's *Sister Carrie* (1900) whose move from town to city creates a loss of innocence and virtue, Carol Kennicott leaves city life for the town, only to discover the hells of Gopher Prairie.

12. Metalious's *Peyton Place* (1956) has been an immensely popular book. The third- and second-place best-seller of 1956 and 1957, its combined paper and hardback sales are the fourth highest of all fiction published between 1895 and 1975 (Hackett and Burke, 1977).

13. Disney's comments are found in Real (1977). For an 'interesting commentary on the relation of Disneyland's Main Street to Disney's own midwestern, boyhood home, see Francaviglia (1976).

Chapter Four: Urban Ideology

1. Sections of this chapter have been previously published in "Urban Views," *Urban Life*, 15, 1 (1986): 3–37, and "Urban Ideology as a Cultural System," *Journal of Cultural Geography*, 5, 2 (1985): 1–15. They are reproduced here with permission of the publishers.

2. For various attempts to characterize American antiurbanism, see Blackwood and Carpenter (1978), Hadden and Barton (1973), White and White (1964), Aronson (1972), Gist and Fava (1964), and Marx (1968).

3. Prourban elements of American culture have received less attention than antiurban themes. See Susman (1985) and Glaab and Brown (1975) for essays that attack the conventional wisdom. Fischer (1984), Strauss (1961), Fries (1977), and Bender (1975) also present evidence indicating that the traditional view of American culture as predominantly antiurban is too simple.

4. Estimates of community preferences vary considerably, depending on the wording of questions. Various surveys are reviewed in Fuguitt and Zuiches (1975) and Zuiches (1981). Estimates in the text are from HUD (1978) and Gallup (1973).

5. Compare, for example, Marans and Rodgers' (1975) account of community satisfaction with Zuiches (1981) review of community preferences.

6. See Becker (1971) for an interesting essay on the origins and sensibility of the culture of civility in San Francisco.

7. This is an apparent reference to "Little Boxes," written by Berkeley folksinger Melvina Reynolds. The chorus runs: "Little boxes on the hillside, little boxes made of ticky-tacky, little boxes on the hillside, little boxes, all the same. There's a pink one and a green one and a blue one and a yellow one, and they're all made out of ticky-tacky and they all look just the same." The song, part of the urbanist critique of suburban uniformity and conformity, was popularized in

the 1960s in a recording by Pete Seeger. This allusion provides a nice example of how an effective community metaphor (suburbs and suburbanites are ticky-tacky), popularized through the mass media, become part of the everyday discourse of contemporary Americans.

Chapter Five: Suburban Ideology

1. For an introduction to recent suburban development and its attendant controversy, see especially Muller (1981), Fischer (1984), and Marsh and Kaplan (1976).

2. See Donaldson (1969), Warner (1962), Hadden and Barton (1973), Meinig (1979) for useful reflections on the ideological sources of the suburban movement in nineteenth- and early twentieth-century American culture.

3. Butler (1976), for instance, takes the reasons that people move to the suburbs literally and, as a result, discusses the causes of suburban growth without mention of white racism.

4. Mills and Gerth (1964) provide a sociological discussion of vocabularies of motives. Here we view a motive, not as an imputed psychological cause of action, but as a standard verbal account that is normally regarded as an adequate and legitimate explanation for a specific personal action.

5. This position does not mean that housing and security are unimportant to Suburbanists or that Suburbanists are, in general, more prejudiced than people who live in other places. It does, however, imply that suburban ideology provides some Suburbanists with a convenient language for masking racial motives.

6. Individuals who moved from another suburb were less likely to mention race as a reason for moving to Hillcrest or Bayside. This suggests another reason why many Suburbanists do not offer racial motives for their move, despite the fact that racial segregation may be important to them. Having lived in a predominantly white community, they assume the next community in which they live will be predominantly white and do not even consider this attribute in their decision-making process.

7. Northern California Community Study, Claude Fischer, Principal Investigator. For the preference data, see the Appendix, Table 5. Information (and the appropriate computer runs) on community designation was kindly supplied by Carol Silverman.

Chapter Six: Community Apologetics

1. Questions on the "friendliness" of community residents appear in various forms in a variety of studies. In a national survey commissioned by the National Rural Electric Cooperative Association, for instance, people were asked whether they felt people would be more likely to be "warm and friendly to other people" in a large city or a rural area. In this highly polarized choice, 7 percent of the American populace chose the city, 81 percent the rural area, and the remainder responded that there was no difference. For other surveys that address this belief at the local or regional level, see Blackwood and Carpenter (1978), Martindale and Hanson (1969), and Buttel and Flinn (1975).

2. See Fischer (1984) for a good summary of the relation between crime and community size. Though Fischer notes that American cities are considerably more dangerous than smaller places in terms of such violent crimes as murder and rape, he also cites evidence that this is by no means universally true. Homicide in Europe and the United States for the nineteenth century and earlier appears more common in rural than urban areas. Moreover, contemporary homicide is more frequent in small communities in the United States than in major cities of other societies, such as Japan. For one interesting study that addresses how contemporary Americans feel about urban disorder and crime, see Wilson (1968).

Chapter Seven: Community Identity

1. This chapter was previously published in an altered form as "City Mouse, Country Mouse: The Persistence of Community Identity," in *Qualitative Sociology*, 9 (1986): 3–25. Printed with permission of the publisher.

2. I assume that individuals actively work to make sense of themselves and the world around them, but they do so under conditions, including symbolic conditions, not of their own making. Community ideologies, thus, are both creative and limiting cultural resources in the construction and rationalization of identity, ones that both open up and close off interpretations of identity. It is quite possible that the formation of community identity, like other forms of identity, is developmentally specific, forming critically at that point in a person's life when identity, more generally, takes form—youth (Erikson, 1980; see Apter, 1964).

3. With the wisdom of hindsight, the prevalence of country people no longer seems so anomalous. Local traditions of the rural

community, the antiurban animus of agrarian ideology, the affilia-
tional character of place identities—all support the use of imageries
of "country life and people" in Valleytown. The relative vitality of this
imagery, however, raises interesting questions about the persistence
and use of such traditionally agrarian themes within the context of a
highly urbanized America. With only tenuous ties to rural experience
or interest, "country life" seems to thrive on other logics. Culturally,
its emphasis on self-reliance, independence, and practicality is
surely nourished by, and in turn reinforces, traditions of American
individualism. Socially, country people in Valleytown were disproportionately working-class Americans, suggesting that country life may
well encode a language of class conflict. Such sources appear
at least consistent with other expressions of "country life" in music,
advertising, and popular icons (country music, Marlboro Men,
pick-up trucks).

4. Survey research studies of community preferences report a
similar phenomenon. Americans disproportionately say they prefer
to live in "small towns," but the majority of such people wish their
"small town" to be within thirty miles of a city, places most social
scientists typically regard as suburbs (Fuguitt and Zuiches, 1975).

5. It should be immediately noted, however, that these individuals who do not identify with a form of community are not entirely
"placeless," lacking any form of place identity. Some describe attachments to the particular community in which they live; most can express nominal preferences for an ideal community. And presumably,
though not directly asked, some identify with other types of places:
favorite rooms, a neighborhood, region, or even "spaceship earth."

Notes: Appendix

1. Some of these conversations have happily become public. See,
for instance, Cuba (1988) and Singleton et al. (1988).

2. Fortunately, research is both a sloppy and a literate activity. It
generates not only data but mountains of written material: notes,
outlines, charts, photocopies, protocols, prospectuses, research
forms, abortive analyses, rough drafts, letters. As much as possible, I
have relied on this material in this account, emphasizing my activities more than my motives.

3. Special thanks are due to Claude Fischer for making these
data available and to Carol Silverman for help with the computer
runs. In my sample, for instance, six-out-of-ten (62%) San Franciscans ideally preferred cities. In the Northern California Commu-

nity Study, residents of central cities selected large (41%) and small (22%) cities at a similar rate. In the Housing and Urban Development national survey of community preferences, 61 percent of residents of large cities (250,000+) preferred to live in a city.

4. This is, of course, an empirical issue and could be fruitfully explored by comparing community beliefs in varied communities of a single type. For instance, though ethnographic literature on small towns suggests considerable uniformity of small-town ideology in quite dissimilar places, more focused analysis might show that the ideology takes different forms in different types of towns: midwestern rural towns versus New England mill towns (see Peshkin 1978; Steinitz and Solomon, 1986).

5. For the creative use of such a sample, see, for instance, Rubin (1976).

6. As Suttles (1984) notes, local ideologies are more likely encountered in older and larger communities, where age nourishes the accumulation of traditions and size enhances institutional support for defended imageries. Yet they are certainly not exclusive to our largest places, as work on Davis, California (Lofland and Lofland, 1987), and Anchorage, Alaska (Cuba, 1987), suggest.

7. That community ideologies involve a physical iconography seems certain. Yet I know of no research that systematically and directly explores how individuals use the built environment to encode alternative ideological presentations of community in daily life. Rapoport (1982a) provides important theoretical groundwork for such a study.

Bibliography

Allen, Irving Lewis, ed. 1977. New Towns and the Suburban Dream. Port Washington, N.Y.: Kennikat Press.

Anderson, Sherwood. 1960. Winesburg, Ohio. New York: Viking Press.

Apter, David, ed. 1964. Ideology and Discontents. Glencoe: Free Press.

Aronson, Sidney. 1972. "The City: Illusion, Nostalgia, and Reality." In Readings in Introductory Sociology, 2nd ed., Dennis Wrong and Harry Gracey, eds. New York: Macmillan.

Becker, Howard, ed. 1971. Culture and Civility in San Francisco. Transaction Books, distributed by Aldine Publishing Company.

Bender, Thomas. 1975. Toward an Urban Vision. Lexington: University Press of Kentucky.

Berger, Bennett. 1960. Working-Class Suburb. Berkeley: University of California Press.

Berger, Peter, and Thomas Luckmann. 1967. The Social Construction of Reality. Garden City, N.Y.: Doubleday.

Berger, Peter, Brigitte Berger, and Hansfried Kellner. 1974. The Homeless Mind: Modernization and Consciousness. New York: Vintage Books.

Blackwood, Larry, and Edwin Carpenter. 1978. "The Importance of Anti-Urbanism in Determining Residential Preferences and Migration Patterns." Rural Sociology, 43: 31–47.

Blakely, Edward, and Ted Bradshaw. 1980. "The Social Economics of the New Rural Migration." Unpublished paper, City and Regional Planning, University of California, Berkeley.

Burton, Virginia Lee. 1942. The Little House. Boston: Houghton Mifflin.

Bushman, Richard. 1970. From Puritan to Yankee. New York: Norton.

Butler, Edgar W. 1976. Urban Sociology. New York: Harper and Row.

Buttel, Frederick, and William Flinn. 1975. "Sources and Consequences of Agrarian Values in American Society." *Rural Sociology*, 40 (Summer): 134–51.

Buttimer, Anne. 1980. "Home, Reach, and the Sense of Place." In The Human Experience of Space and Place, Ann Buttimer and David Seamon, eds. New York: St. Martin's Press.

Campbell, Agnus. 1981. The Sense of Well-Being in America: Recent Patterns and Trends. New York: McGraw-Hill.

————. 1971. White Attitudes toward Black People. Institute for Social Research, Ann Arbor, University of Michigan.

Campbell, Agnus, Phillip Converse, and Willard Rodgers. 1976. The Quality of American Life. New York: Russell Sage.

Canter, David. 1977. The Psychology of Place. New York: St. Martin's Press.

Castells, Manuel. 1983. The City and The Grass Roots. Berkeley: University of California Press.

Christenson, James. 1979. "Urbanism and Community Sentiment." *Social Science Quarterly*, 60 (3): 387–400.

Cochrance, Timothy. 1987. "Place, People, and Folklore: An Isle Royale Case Study." *Western Folklore*, 46 (1): 1–20.

Coles, Robert. 1967. Migrants, Sharecroppers, and Mountaineers. Boston: Little, Brown.

Cooper, Clare. 1974. "The House as a Symbol of Self." In Designing for Human Behavior, Jon Lang et al., eds. Stroudsburg, Pa.: Dowden, Hutchinson, and Ross.

Csikzentmihalyi, Mihaly, and Eugene Rochberg-Halton. 1981. The Meaning of Things: Domestic Symbols and the Self. Cambridge: Cambridge University Press.

Cuba, Lee. 1988. A Short Guide to Writing about Social Science. Glenview, Ill.: Scott, Foresman.

————. 1987. Identity and Community on the Alaskan Frontier. Philadelphia: Temple University Press.

————. 1984. "Reorientations of Self: Residential Identification in Anchorage, Alaska." Studies in Symbolic Interaction, volume 5, 219–37.

DeJong, Gordon G., and Relph Sell. 1977. "Population Redistribution, Migration, and Residential Preferences." *Annals*, AAPSS, 429 (January): 130–44.

Dillman, Don A. 1979. "Residential Preferences, Quality of Life, and the Population Turnaround." *American Journal of Agricultural Economics*, 61: 960–66.

Dillman, Don, and Daryl Hobbs, eds. 1982. Rural Society in the U.S. Boulder: Westview Press.

Dillman, Don, and Kenneth Tremblay. 1977. "The Quality of Life in rural America." *Annals*, AAPSS, 429 (January): 115–29.

Dobriner, William M. 1963. Class in Suburbia. Englewood Cliffs, N.J.: Prentice-Hall.

Dolce, Philip, ed. 1976. Suburbia: The American Dream and Dilemma. Garden City, N.Y.: Anchor.

Donaldson, Scott. 1969. The Suburban Myth. New York: Columbia University Press.

Dreiser, Theodore. [1900] 1932. Sister Carrie. New York: Modern Library.

Duncan, James. 1973. "Landscape Taste as a Symbol of Group Identity." *Geographical Review*, 63: 334–55.

Duncan, James, ed. 1982. Housing and Identity. New York: Holmes and Meier.

Durkheim, Emile. 1969. The Division of Labor in Society. New York: Free Press.

Engels, Fredrick. 1968. The Condition of the Working Class in England. Stanford: Stanford University Press.

Erikson, Erik. 1980. Identity and the Life Cycle. New York: Norton.

Erikson, Kai. 1976. Everything in It's Path. New York: Simon and Schuster.

Fava, Sylvia. 1985. "Suburban Era: A New Look?" *Sociological Focus*, 18 (2): 109–17.

———. 1973. "The Pop Sociology of Suburbs and New Towns." *American Studies*, 14 (Spring): 121–33.

Fava, Sylvia, and Judith Desena. 1984. "The Chosen Apple: Young Suburban Migrants." In The Apple Sliced: Sociological Studies of New York City, V. Boggs, G. Handel, and S. Fava, eds. New York: Praeger.

Fischer, Claude. 1984. The Urban Experience, 2nd ed. New York: Harcourt Brace Jovanovich.

————. 1982. To Dwell Among Friends: Personal Networks in Town and City. Chicago: University of Chicago Press.

————. 1977. "Comments on the History and Study of Community." In Networks and Places, Fischer et al. New York: Free Press.

Fischer, Claude S. et al. 1977. Networks and Places. New York: Free Press.

Fischer, Claude S., and C. Ann Stueve. 1977. " 'Authentic Community': The Role of Place in Modern Life." In Networks and Places, Claude Fischer et al. New York: Free Press.

Francaviglia, Richard V. 1976. "Main Street U.S.A.: The Creation of a Popular Image." Unpublished paper presented at the annual meeting of the Popular Culture Association, Chicago, April 23.

Frederickson, Carl, Glenn V. Fuguitt, Tim Heaton, and James Zuiches. 1979. "Residential Preferences, Community Satisfaction, and the Intention to Move." Demography, 16: 565–73.

Freidel, Frank. 1963. "Boosters, Intellectuals, and the American City." In The Historian and the City, O. Handlin and J. Burchard, eds. Cambridge, Mass.: MIT and Harvard Press.

Fried, Marc. 1982. "Residential Attachment: Sources of Residential and Community Satisfaction." Journal of Social Issues, 38 (3): 107–19.

————. 1963. "Grieving for a Lost Home." In The Urban Condition, L. J. Duhl, ed. New York: Basic Books.

Fried, Marc, and Peggy Gleicher. 1961. "Some Sources of Residential Satisfaction in an Urban Slum." Journal of the American Institute of Planners, 27 (no. 4, November).

Fries, Sylvia D. 1977. The Urban Idea in Colonial America. Philadelphia: Temple University Press.

Fuguitt, Glenn, and James Zuiches. 1975. "Residential Preferences and Population Distribution." Demography, 12: 491–504.

Furay, Conal. 1977. The Grass-Roots Mind in America: The American Sense of Absolutes. New York: New Viewpoints.

Gale, Zona. 1909. Friendship Village Love Stories. New York: Macmillan.

Gallup Opinion Index. 1973. "Ideal Place to Live?" April, no. 94: 31.

————. 1971. "Living Preferences." August, no. 74: 28.

Gans, Herbert J. 1968. "The White Exodus to Suburbia Steps Up." *The New York Times Magazine*, January 7.

————. 1967. The Levittowners. New York: Vintage Books.

————. 1962. The Urban Villagers. New York: Free Press.

Geertz, Clifford. 1973. The Interpretation of Cultures: Selected Essays. New York: Basic Books.

Gelfant, Blanche. 1954. The American City Novel. Norman: University of Oklahoma Press.

Gerson, Elihu M., and M. Sue Gerson. 1976. "The Social Framework of Place Perspectives." In Environmental Knowing, G. T. Moore and R. G. Golledge, eds. Stroudsburg, Pa.: Dowden, Hutchinson, and Ross.

Gerson, Kathleen, C. Ann Stueve, and Claude Fischer. 1977. "Attachment to Place." In Networks and Places, C. Fischer et al. New York: Free Press.

Gist, Noel, and Sylvia Fava. 1964. Urban Society. New York: Thomas Crowell.

Glaab, Charles N., and A. Theodore Brown. 1975. "The City in American Thought, 1790–1850." In A History of Urban America. New York: Macmillan.

Glaser, Barney, and Anselm Strauss. 1967. The Discovery of Grounded Theory. Chicago: Aldine Publishing Company.

Goist, Park Dixon. 1977. From Main Street to State Street. Port Washington, N.Y.: Kennikat Press.

Goldman, Robert, and David Dickens. 1983. "The Selling of Rural America." *Rural Sociology*, 48: 585–606.

Goleman, Daniel. 1985. "Scientists Find City is a Series of Varying Perceptions." *The New York Times* (December 31): C1 and C6.

Gould, Peter, and Rodney White. 1986. Mental Maps, 2nd ed. Boston: Allen & Unwin.

Greeley, Andrew M., and Paul Sheatsley. 1973. "Attitudes Toward Racial Integration." In Cities, Kingsley Davis, ed. San Francisco: W. H. Freeman.

Guest, Avery M., and Barrett A. Lee. 1983a. "Consensus on Locality Names within the Metropolis." *Sociology and Social Research*, 67 (4): 374–91.

Guest, Avery M., and Barrett A. Lee. 1983b. "Sentiment and Evaluation as Ecological Variables." *Sociological Perspectives*, 26 (2): 159–84.

Guest, Avery M., Barrett Lee, and Lyn Stacheli. 1982. "Changing Locality Identification in the Metropolis: Seattle, 1920–78." *American Sociological Review*, 47 (August): 543–49.

Gusfield, Joseph. 1978. Community: A Critical Response. New York: Harper and Row.

Haar, Charles. 1972. The End of Innocence. Glenview, Ill.: Scott, Foresman.

Hackett, Alice, and James Burke. 1977. 80 Years of Best Sellers: 1895–1975. New York: Bowker.

Hadden, Jeffrey K., and Josef J. Barton. 1973. "An Image that Will Not Die: Thoughts on the History of Anti-Urban Ideology." In The Urbanization of the Suburbs, L. H. Masotti and J. K. Hadden, eds. Volume 7, Urban Affairs Annual Reviews. Beverly Hills: Sage Publications.

Harvey, David. 1985a. "Money, Time, Space, and the City." In Consciousness and the Urban Experience. Baltimore: Johns Hopkins University Press.

———. 1985b. "The Urbanization of Consciousness." In Consciousness and the Urban Experience. Baltimore: Johns Hopkins University Press.

Hawley, Amos, and Sara Mazie. 1981. "An Overview." In Nonmetropolitan America in Transition, A. Hawley and S. Mazie, eds. Chapel Hill: University of North Carolina Press. 3–23.

Hewitt, John. 1984. Self and Society, 3rd ed. Boston: Allyn and Bacon.

Hofstadter, Richard. 1955. The Age of Reform. New York: Vintage Books.

Howard, Maureen. 1986. "I Could Not Tell You Where I Came From: Going Home to Bridgeport." *New England Monthly* (June): 49–50.

Howell, Frank, and Wolfgang Frese. 1983. "Size of Place, Residential Preferences, and the Life Cycle: How People Come to Like Where They Live." *American Sociological Review*, 48: 569–80.

HUD, United States Department of Housing and Urban Development. 1978. A Survey of Citizen Views and Concerns about Urban Life. Study no. P2795.

————. nd. The 1978 HUD Survey on the Quality of Community Life: Data Book. Data collected by Louis Harris and Associates.

Hummon, David M. 1989. "House, Home, and Identity in Contemporary American Culture." In Housing, Culture, and Design, Setha Low and Erve Chambers, eds. Philadelphia: University of Pennsylvania Press.

————. 1988. "Tourist Worlds: Tourist Advertising, Ritual, and American Culture." *Sociological Quarterly*, 29 (2): 179–202.

————. 1986a. "City Mouse, Country Mouse: The Persistence of Community Identity." *Qualitative Sociology*, 9 (1): 3–25.

————. 1986b. "Urban Views: Popular Perspectives on City Life." *Urban Life*, 15 (1): 3–37.

————. 1986c. "Place Identities: Localities of the Self." In Purposes in Built Form and Culture Research, J. William Carswell and David Saile, eds. Proceedings of the 1986 International Conference on Built Form and Culture Research, University of Kansas Press. 34–37.

————. 1985. "Urban Ideology as a Cultural System." *Journal of Cultural Geography*, 5 (2): 1–16.

————. 1980. "Popular Images of the American Small Town." *Landscape*, 24: 3–9.

Hunter, Albert. 1978. "Persistence of Local Sentiments in Mass Society." In Handbook of Urban Life, D. Street, ed. San Francisco: Jossey-Bass. 133–62.

————. 1974. Symbolic Communities. Chicago: University of Chicago Press.

Karp, David, Gregory Stone, and William Yoels. 1977. Being Urban. Lexington, Mass.: D. C. Heath.

Kasarda, John, and Morris Janowitz. 1974. "Community Attachment in Mass Society." *American Sociological Review*, 39 (June): 28–39.

Keesing, Roger. 1981. "Theories of Culture." In Language, Culture, and Cognition, Ronald Casson, ed. New York: MacMillan.

Keillor, Garrison. 1985. Lake Wobegon Days. New York: Viking Press.

Klapp, Orin. 1969. Collective Search for Identity. New York: Holt, Rinehart, and Winston.

Kornblum, William. 1974. Blue Collar Community. Chicago: University of Chicago Press.

Krase, Jerome. 1979. "Stigmatized Places, Stigmatized People: Crown Heights and Prospect-Lefferts Gardens." In Brooklyn USA: The Fourth Largest City in America, Rita Seiden Miller, ed. New York: Brooklyn College Press.

Kristol, Irving. 1970. "Urban Civilization and Its Discontents." Commentary (July): 29–35.

Krupat, Edward. 1985. People in Cities. New York: Cambridge University Press.

La Gory, Mark, and John Pipkin. 1981. Urban Social Space. Belmont, Calif.: Wadsworth Publishing Company.

Lane, Roger. 1968. "Urbanization and Criminal Violence in the Nineteenth Century." The Journal of Social History, 2 (2): 156–63.

Langer, Peter. 1984. "Sociology—Four Images of Organized Diversity: Bazaar, Jungle, Organism, and Machine." In Cities of the Mind, Lloyd Rodwin and Robert Hollister, eds. New York: Plenum Press. 97–118.

Lapham, Lewis. 1976. "City Lights." Harpers (June): 8–14.

Lee, Barrett A. 1983. "Determinants of Neighborhood Satisfaction: A Metropolitan-Level Analysis." The Sociological Quarterly, 24: 287–303.

Lerner, Max. 1957. America as a Civilization. New York: Simon and Schuster.

Lewis, Sinclair. 1920. Mainstreet. New York: Harcourt, Brace and Company.

Lingeman, Richard. 1980. Small Town America: A Narrative History, 1620–Present. Boston: Houghton Mifflin.

Lockridge, Kenneth. 1970. A New England Town. New York: Norton.

Lofland, Lyn. 1973. A World of Strangers. New York: Basic Books.

————. Communication and Construction: The Built Environment as Message and Medium. Forthcoming in Information, Communication, and Social Structure, David Maines and Carl Couch, eds. Springfield, Ill.: Charles C. Thomas.

Lofland, John, and Lyn Lofland. 1987. "Lime Politics: The Selectively Progressive Ethos of Davis, California." Research in Political Sociology, 3: 245–68.

Lohof, Bruce. 1983. "The Higher Meaning of Marlboro Cigarettes." In The Popular Culture Reader, 3rd ed., C. Geist and J. Nachbar, eds. Bowling Green: Bowling Green University Press.

Lowenthal, David, and M. Riel. 1972. Milieu and Observer Differences in Environmental Associations. Publications in Environmental Perception, no. 7. New York: American Geographical Society.

Lynch, Kevin. 1960. The Image of the City. Cambridge: MIT Press.

———. 1984. "Reconsidering the Image of the City." In Cities of the Mind, Lloyd Rodwin and Robert Hollister, eds. New York: Plenum Press. 151–62.

Lynd, Robert, and Helen Lynd. 1929. Middletown. New York: Harcourt, Brace and World.

MacCannell, Dean. 1976. The Tourist. New York: Schocken Books.

Marans, Robert W., and Willard Rodgers. 1975. "Toward an Understanding of Community Satisfaction." In Metropolitan America in Contemporary Perspective, A. Hawley and V. Rock, eds. New York: John Wiley.

Marcus, Steven. 1975. Engels, Manchester, and the Working-Class. New York: Vintage Books.

Marsh, Margaret, and Samuel Kaplan. 1976. "The Lure of the Suburbs." In Suburbia, Philip Dolce, ed. Garden City, N. Y.: Anchor Books.

Martin, Judith. 1979. Miss Manner's Guide to Excruciatingly Correct Behavior. New York: Warner.

Martindale, Don, and R. Galen Hanson. 1969. Small Town and the Nation. Westport, Conn.: Greenwood Publishing Company.

Marx, Karl. 1972. The Marx-Engels Reader, Robert Tucker, ed. New York: Norton.

Marx, Leo. 1984. "The Puzzle of Antiurbanism in Classic American Literature." In Cities of the Mind, Lloyd Rodwin and Robert Hollister, eds. New York: Plenum Press. 163–80.

———. 1968. "Pastoral Ideals and City Troubles." In The Fitness of Man's Environment, Smithsonian Annual II. Washington, D.C.: Smithsonian Institution Press.

Masters, Edgar Lee. 1915. Spoon River Anthology. New York: Macmillan.

Mazie, Sara Mills, and Steve Rawlings. 1972. "Public Attitude Towards Population Distribution Issues." In Commission on Population Growth and the American Future, Research Reports, volume 5, Population Distribution and Policy, S. M. Mazie, ed. Washington, D.C.: Government Printing Office. 603–15.

Meinig, Donald W. 1979. "Symbolic Landscapes: Some Idealizations of American Communities." In The Interpretation of Ordinary Landscapes: Geographical Essays, Donald W. Meinig, ed. New York: Oxford University Press. 135–45.

Metalious, Grace. 1956. Peyton Place. New York: Dell books.

Michelson, William. 1980. "Long and Short Range Criteria for Housing Choice and Environmental Behavior." Journal of Social Issues, 36: 135–49.

Milgram, Stanley. 1970. "The Experience of Living in Cities." Science, 167 (March 13): 1461–68.

Milich, Nick. 1987. "Nigger Heaven." The Davis Enterprise (Sunday, September 20): 25, 29.

Miller, F. D., S. Tsemberis, G. P. Malia, and D. Grega. 1980. "Neighborhood Satisfaction among Urban Dwellers." Journal of Social Issues, 36 (3): 101–17.

Mills, C. Wright, and Hans Gerth. 1964 [1953]. Character and Social Structure. New York: Harcourt, Brace and World.

Moon, William Least Heat. 1982. Blue Highways. Boston: Little, Brown.

Moore, Gary. 1979. "Knowing about Environmental Knowing: The Current State of Theory and Research about Environmental Cognition." Environment and Behavior, 11: 33–70.

Muller, Peter O. 1981. Contemporary Suburban America. Englewood Cliffs, N.J.: Prentice-Hall.

Nachbar, Jack. 1983. "Culture and Continuity: Three Myths in the Prints of Currier and Ives." In The Popular Culture Reader, 3rd ed., C. Geist and J. Nachbar, eds. Bowling Green: Bowling Green University Press.

National Rural Electric Cooperative Association. 1968. The Nation's View of Rural America and Rural Electrification. Pamphlet prepared by the International Research Associates.

Newsweek. 1981. "The Small Town Boom." (July 6): 26–37.

Nisbet, R. A. 1969. The Quest for Community. New York: Oxford University Press.

Packard, Vance. 1972. A Nation of Strangers. New York: McKay.

Palin, John. 1981. City Scenes, 2nd ed. Boston: Little, Brown.

Perin, Constance. 1977. Everything in Its Place. Princeton, N.J.: Princeton University Press.

Peshkin, Alan. 1978. Growing Up American. Chicago: University of Chicago Press.

Pinkwater, Daniel. 1977. The Big Orange Splot. New York: Hastings House.

Rabinow, Paul. 1977. Reflections on Fieldwork in Morocco. Berkeley: University of California Press.

Rapoport, Amos. 1982a. "Identity and Environment." In Housing and Identity, James Duncan, ed. New York: Holmes and Meier.

————. 1982b. The Meaning of the Built Environment. Beverly Hills: Sage Publications.

————. 1980. "Environmental Preference, Habitat Selection, and Urban Housing." *Journal of Social Issues*, 36: 118–34.

————. 1977. Human Aspects of Urban Form. New York: Pergamon Press.

Real, Michael. 1977. Mass-Mediated Culture. Englewood Cliffs, N.J.: Prentice-Hall.

Reed, John Shelton. 1983. Southerners: The Social Psychology of Sectionalism. Chapel Hill: University of North Carolina Press.

Relph, Edward. 1976. Place and Placelessness. London: Pion.

Reiss, A. J. 1959. "Rural-Urban and Status Differences in Interpersonal Contacts." *American Journal of Sociology*, 65 (September): 182–95.

Rivlin, Leanne. 1982. "Group Membership and Place Meanings in an Urban Neighborhood." *Journal of Social Issues*, 38 (3): 75–93.

Rodgers, Willard. 1980. "Residential Satisfaction in Relationship to Size of Place." *Social Psychology Quarterly*, 43 (4): 436–41.

Rodwin, Lloyd, and Robert Hollister, eds. 1984. Cities of the Mind: Images and Themes of the City in the Social Sciences. New York: Plenum Press.

Rourke, Francis E. 1964. "Urbanism and American Democracy." *Ethics*, 74 (July): 255–68.

Rowles, G. D. 1983a. "Place and Personal Identity in Old Age: Observations from Appalachia." *Journal of Environmental Psychology*, 3: 299–313.

————. 1983b. "Exploring the Meaning of Place in Old Age." Paper presented at the 36th annual meeting of the Gerontological Society of America, San Francisco, November 21.

Rubin, Lillian. 1976. Worlds of Pain: Life in the Working-Class Family. New York: Basic Books.

Rutman, Darrett. 1965. Winthrop's Boston. New York: Norton.

Schwartz, Barry. 1976. "Images of Suburbia: Some Revisionist Commentary and Conclusions." In The Changing Face of the Suburbs, Barry Schwartz, ed. Chicago: University of Chicago Press.

Schorske, Carl E. 1968. "The Idea of the City in European Thought: Voltaire to Spengler." In Urbanism in World Perspective, S. F. Fava, ed. New York: Thomas Y. Crowell.

Schrag, Peter. 1972. "Is Main Street Still There?" In Life Styles, S. D. Feldman and G. W. Thielbar, eds. Boston: Little, Brown.

Seamon, David. 1979. A Geography of the Lifeworld. New York: St. Martin's Press.

Seeley, J. R., R. A. Sim, and E. W. Loosley. 1956. Crestwood Heights. Toronto: University of Toronto Press.

Shibutani, Tamotsu. 1955. "Reference Groups as Perspectives." *American Journal of Sociology*, 60 (May): 562–69.

Silverman, Carol. 1983. "Community in America." Manuscript from dissertation, Berkeley, University of California.

Singleton, Jr., Royce, Bruce Straits, Margaret Straits, and Ronald McAllister. 1988. Approaches to Social Research. New York: Oxford University Press.

Smith, Page. 1966. As a City upon a Hill: The Town in American History. Cambridge: MIT Press.

Stein, Benjamin. 1976. "Whatever Happened to Small-town America?" *The Public Interest*, 44 (Summer): 17–26.

Stein, Maurice. 1960. The Eclipse of Community. Princeton. N.J.: Princeton University Press.

Steinitz, Victoria, and Ellen Solomon. 1986. Starting Out: Class and Community in the Lives of Working-Class Youth. Philadelphia: Temple University Press.

Stoneall, Linda. 1983. "Where Are You From? A Case of Rural Residential Identification." *Qualitative Sociology*, 6: 51–65.

Strauss, Anselm. 1971. The Contexts of Social Mobility: Ideology and Theory. Chicago: Aldine Publishing Company.

————. 1968. "Urban Perspectives: New York City." In The American City. Chicago: Aldine Publishing Company.

————. 1961. Images of the American City. New York: Free Press.

Susman, Warren. 1985. Culture as History. New York: Pantheon Books.

Suttles, Gerald. 1984. "The Cumulative Texture of Local Urban Culture." *American Journal of Sociology*, 90 (2): 283–302.

————. 1972. The Social Construction of Communities. Chicago: University of Chicago Press.

————. 1968. The Social Order of the Slum. Chicago: University of Chicago Press.

Tuan, Yi-Fu. 1980. "Rootedness versus Sense of Place." *Landscape*, 24 (1), 3–8.

————. 1977. Space and Place: The Perspective of Experience. Minneapolis: University of Minnesota Press.

————. 1974. Topophilia. Englewood Cliffs, N.J.: Prentice Hall.

Tunley, Roul. 1977. "Comeback of the Small Town." *Reader's Digest* (October): 143–47.

U.S. Bureau of the Census. 1987. Statistical Abstract of the United States, 1988 (108th edition). Washington, D.C.

————. Census of the Population, 1970, volume 1, Characteristics of the Population, Part 6, California—Section 1.

Vidich, Arthur, and Joseph Bensman. 1960. Small Town in Mass Society. Princeton, N.J.: Princeton University Press.

Warner, Sam. 1984. "Slums and Skyscrapers: Urban Images, Symbols, and Ideology." In Cities of the Mind, Lloyd Rodwin and Robert Hollister, eds. New York: Plenum Press. 181–96.

————. 1962. Street Car Suburbs. Cambridge: Harvard University Press.

Webber, Mel. 1970. "Order in Diversity." In Neighborhood, City and Metropolis, R. Gutman and D. Popenoe, eds. New York: Random House. 792–811.

Weber, Max. 1958. The City. New York: Free Press.

———. 1946. From Max Weber: Essays in Sociology, H. Gerth and C. W. Mills, eds. New York: Oxford University Press.

Weigert, Andrew. 1981. Sociology of Everyday Life. New York: Longman.

West, Nathanael. 1962. Miss Lonelyhearts and The Day of the Locust. New York: A New Directions Paperback.

Wheelis, Allen. 1958. The Quest for Identity. New York: Norton.

White, Morton, and Lucia White. 1964. The Intellectual versus the City: From Thomas Jefferson to Frank Lloyd Wright. New York: New American Library.

Whyte, William Foote. 1955. Street Corner Society. Chicago: University of Chicago Press.

Whyte, Jr., William H. 1957. The Organization Man. Garden City, N.Y.: Anchor Books.

Williams, Raymond. 1973. The Country and the City. New York: Oxford University Press.

Wilson, James Q. 1968. "The Urban Unease." The Public Interest, 12 (Summer): 25–39.

Wirt, Frederick. 1974. Power in the City. Berkeley: University of California Press.

Wirth, Louis. 1938. "Urbanism as a Way of Life." American Journal of Sociology, 44 (July): 1–24.

Wohl, R., and A. Strauss. 1958. "Symbolic Representation and the Urban Milieu." American Journal of Sociology, 63: 523–32.

Wright, Will. 1975. Sixguns and Society: A Structural Study of the Western. Berkeley: University of California Press.

Wrong, Dennis H. 1972. "Suburbs and Myths of Suburbia." In Readings in Introductory Sociology, 2nd ed., D. Wrong and H. Gracey, eds. New York: Macmillan.

Young, Michael, and Peter Willmott. 1957. Family and Kinship in East London. Glencoe, Ill.: Free Press.

Zeisel, John. 1984. Inquiry by Design. Cambridge: Cambridge University Press.

————. 1973. "Symbolic Meaning of Space and the Physical Dimension of Social Relations." In Cities in Change, J. Walton and D. Carns, eds. Boston: Allyn and Bacon.

Zelan, Joseph. 1968. "Does Suburbia Make a Difference?" In Urbanism in World Perspective, Sylvia Fava, ed. New York: Thomas Crowell.

Zuiches, James J. 1982. "Residential Preferences." In Rural Society in the U.S.: Issues for the 1980s, Don A. Dillman and Daryl J. Hobbs, eds. Boulder, Colo.: Westview. 247–55.

————. 1981. "Residential Preferences in the United States." In Nonmetropolitan America in Transition, A. Hawley and S. Mills, eds. Chapel Hill: University of North Carolina Press.

————. 1980. "Residential Preferences in Migration Theory." In New Directions in Urban-Rural Migration Research, David L. Brown and John M. Wardwell, eds. New York: Academic Press. 163–88.

Zuiches, James J., and Glenn V. Fuguitt. 1972. "Residential Preferences: Implications for Population Redistribution in Nonmetropolitan Areas." Commission on Population Growth and the American Future, Research Reports, volume 5, Population Distribution and Policy, S. M. Mazie, ed. Washington, D.C.: Government Printing Office.

Zuiches, James J., and Jon H. Rieger. 1978. "Size of Place Preferences and Life Cycle Migration: A Cohort Comparison." *Rural Sociology*, 43: 618–33.

Index

Rubin, Lillian, 211n.5
Rural life: and agrarianism, 34–35;
and small-town imagery, 65–66;
and country identity, 151–56
Rutman, Darrett, 129

Safety and Crime: and community
size, 209n.2; in opinion surveys,
31; in small-town ideology, 58–59,
60, 129–33; in suburban ideology,
103; in urban ideology, 133–38
Sample communities, 40–41, 186–
87, 188, 197, 204n.16. *See also*
Methodology
San Francisco, 40–41, 204–5n.16,
207n.6
Satisfaction. *See* Community satis-
faction
Schrag, Peter, 50
Schwartz, Barry, 97
Schorske, Carl E., 202n.6
Seamon, David, 144, 203n.7
Self-conception and community
identity, 143, 148–57, 162–63
Sell, Relph, 30, 205n.3
Sentiment. *See* Community sentiment
Sheatsley, Paul, 107
Shibutani, Tamotsu, 11
Silverman, Carol, 208n.7, 210–11n.3
Simplicity, images of, 172–74; in
small-town ideology, 68; in urban
ideology, 91–92
Singleton, Royce, Jr., 210n.1
Sister Carrie, 206n.11
Size, community: and community
accounts, 123–24, 130; and crime,
209n.2; and designation of town, 82
Slum, images of, 35–36
Small Town, 65
Small town, the: identification with,
148–51; in literature, 3, 66, 201n.1,
206n.11; popularity of, 47–50; in
small-town ideology, 52–59; in
suburban ideology, 103–105; in
urban ideology, 82–85
Small-town ideology: and images of
the city, 59–63; and images of the
town, 52–59; and images of the
suburb, 63–65; as symbolic landscape, 65–68, 170

Small-town people, images of, 148–49
Smith, Page, 3, 66, 206n.10
Social change: and community imagery, 35–36, 66–67; and place consciousness, 4; and the town, 65–
67; and suburbia, 95–96; versus
tradition, 35
Social class: and community prefer-
ences, 32; and community satis-
faction, 22; and mental maps, 19;
and sample design, 41, 186–87, 188
Social ties and community attach-
ment, 25–26
Socialization and community prefer-
ences, 30
Solomon, Ellen, 25, 211n.5
Spatial environment: mental maps of,
17–20; local culture and, xiii–xiv, 28
Stein, Maurice, 141, 167
Steinitz, Victoria, 25, 211n.5
Stigma and community belief, 28,
159, 204n.11
Stone, Gregory, 27, 142
Straits, Bruce, 210n.1
Straits, Margaret, 210n.1
Street Corner Society, 183
Stueve, C. Ann, 25, 26
Susman, Warren, 34, 207n.3
Suburb: as "best of both worlds," 98,
110–11, 114, 180–81; conflicting
interpretations of, 114–16; identification with the, 155–57; as middle
landscape, 180–81; in small-town
ideology, 63–65, 115; in suburban
ideology, 98–103; in urban ideology, 86–91, 115; as "worst of both
worlds," 86
Suburban folk as identity, 155–57
Suburban ideology: attenuated imagery of, 98, 115–16, 157–59; the
city in, 103–105; the town in, 103–
105; the suburb in, 98–103; vocabularies of motive in, 108–109;
white flight and, 105–109
Suburban myth, the, 96
Suburbanists, 42–43, 98
Suttles, Gerald, 15, 27, 142, 203n.9,
204n.15, 211n.6
Symbolic landscape, 39; and community perspective, 172; of small-

town ideology, 65–68; of suburban
ideology, 114; of urban ideology,
91–92
Symbolic locale, place as, 9, 33–36

Talk about communities: and meth-
odology, 185; reasons for, xiii–xiv
Tolerance, images of: in community
identity, 151; in community ideol-
ogy, 80–81, 89–90, 177
Town folk, 148–51
Tradition: in community ideology,
85, 174, 176–77; versus social
change, 35
Tremblay, Kenneth, 8, 22, 49
Tsemberis, S., 23
Tuan, Yi-Fu, 17, 27, 34, 74, 201n.2,
202n.2, 203n.7, 204n.15
Tunley, Roul, 47, 58

United States Bureau of Census, 31
Urban ideology, 70; as landscape,
91–92; as perspective, 93–94; and
small-town images, 82–85; and
suburban images, 86–91; and urban images, 75–81; and urban
problems, 120–21
Urban migrants, 30, 73
Urban problems: public opinion and,
48, 119–20; urban ideology and,
120. See also Community
accounts; Community problems
Urban versus rural life, 35
Urbanists, 42–43; and the city, 71; in
suburbia, 109, 112–13; temporary, 73
Urbanites, reluctant, 71–74

Valleytown, 51–52
Values and American culture, 168;
as community versus individual,
174–75; as conservatism versus

liberalism, 174, 176–77; as periphery versus centrality, 177–79; as
simplicity versus complexity, 172–
74; as tradition versus modernity,
174, 176–77
Values and community ideology, 40,
145–46, 167–68
Vidich, Arthur, 24, 50, 66, 67, 155,
206n.8
Villagers, 42–43, 109–112

Warner, Sam, 35, 204n.14, 208n.2
Webber, Mel, 141
Weber, Max, 24
West, Nathanael, 119
Wheelis, Allen, 141
White, Morton, 34, 207n.2
White, Lucia, 34, 207n.2
White, Rodney, 19, 202n.2
White flight, 99, 105–109
Whyte, William F., 183
Whyte, William H., Jr., 96
Williams, Raymond, 35, 202n.6
Willmott, Peter, 25
Wilson, James Q., 209n.1
Wirt, Frederick, 204–5n.16
Wirth, Louis, 24, 141
Work and the city: in community
ideology, 63, 77, 78; in public opin-
ion, 30, 31
Wright, Will, 206n.5
Wrong, Dennis H., 97

Yoels, William, 27, 142
Young, Michael, 25

Zeisel, John, 202n.3
Zelan, Joseph, 30, 32
Zuiches, James, 29, 30, 31, 32, 69,
97, 207n.4, 207n.5, 210n.4